D0308020

SPINDLE RIVER

**Other Cambridge Reading books
you may enjoy**

Sorcery and Gold
Rosalind Kerven

The Hermit Shell
Frances Usher

Sandstorm
Judy Cumberbatch

Heroes and Villains
edited by Tony Bradman

**Other books by Judith O'Neill
you may enjoy**

So Far from Skye

Hearing Voices

Stringybark Summer

The Message

Spindle River

Judith O'Neill

Illustrated by Ian Stephens

CAMBRIDGE
UNIVERSITY PRESS

Cambridge Reading

General Editors
Richard Brown and Kate Ruttle

Consultant Editor
Jean Glasberg

PUBLISHED BY THE PRESS SYNDICATE OF THE UNIVERSITY OF CAMBRIDGE
The Pitt Building, Trumpington Street, Cambridge, United Kingdom

CAMBRIDGE UNIVERSITY PRESS
The Edinburgh Building, Cambridge CB2 2RU, UK   http://www.cup.cam.ac.uk
40 West 20th Street, New York, NY 10011-4211, USA   http://www.cup.org.
10 Stamford Road, Oakleigh, Melbourne 3166, Australia
Ruiz de Alarcón 13, 28014 Madrid, Spain

Text © Judith O'Neill 1998
Illustrations © Ian Stephens 1998
Cover illustration © Paul Catherall 1998

This book is in copyright. Subject to statutory exception and to the provisions of
relevant collective licensing agreements, no reproduction of any part may take
place without the written permission of Cambridge University Press.

First published 1998
Reprinted 1999

Printed in the United Kingdom at the University Press, Cambridge

Typeface Concorde   *System* QuarkXPress®

A catalogue record for this book is available from the British Library

ISBN 0 521 47629 1   paperback

This book is dedicated to my friends
Nicholas and Rosemary Boyle
and to their children
Mary, Michael, Doran and Angela.

Acknowledgements

The author would like to thank all the people who have helped her with information, ideas, advice and encouragement: Lorna Davidson, Education Officer of the New Lanark Conservation Trust; Dr Ian Donnachie of the Open University in Scotland, historian of New Lanark; John Darbyshire and Jane Chalmers of the Scottish Wildlife Trust, Falls of Clyde Reserve; Vincent Newton and Bob Holden of the Museum of Science and Industry in Manchester; Ian Lafferty of the Lothian and Borders Fire Brigade; the Revd John W M Cameron; Professor Ian Campbell; Humphrey Errington; Joy Hendry; Mairi Robinson; Margaret Sutherland; Jean Wallace; and the members of staff at the New Lanark Mills, the National Library of Scotland, the Royal Museum of Scotland, the Glasgow University Archives, and at Quarry Bank Mill, Styal, Cheshire. In particular she thanks her husband, John, who went with her so often to New Lanark and who shares her love of the place.

Contents

CHAPTER 1

Coming to the Mills

Lanark, Scotland, July 1819

"Whoa there!"

The carter reined in his horses abruptly at the top end of Lanark's High Street. He'd been glad to let the family from the far north ride on his cart for these last ten miles but now his own journey was almost at an end.

"Ye'll have to jump doun here," he called back to them where they sat perched on his load of bulging sacks. "I'm stoppin off in the Old Toun for a while. My horses are wantin their corn and I'm ready for a bite o' bread and cheese mysel. Ye'll get to the mills far sooner if ye walk. Just ask onybody the way."

The mother slid to the ground first with little Davie still asleep in her arms.

"Thank ye for bringin us so far," she said to the carter, smiling up at him from a tired, sun-browned face. She was a fine-looking woman of only thirty-five but there were early streaks of grey in her hair and lines of sorrow on her cheeks.

The smile faded quickly as her anxious eyes stared out at this strange, lowland town. She saw the closely packed row of houses on each side of a long, sloping street. She saw the tall church with its clock tower down at the far end. With a sudden shout of relief, her four older children – Henny and Jockie, Betty and Tam – sprang together from the cart, laughing as they leapt, each one of them clutching a bundle from home.

The minute her feet touched the ground, Henny had one of those strange moments when she remembered her father. She hadn't given him a thought all that morning, but now, in an instant, his face seemed startlingly clear to her again and his kind eyes shone down at her. It was almost as if he were there beside her in the long Lanark street. With the sudden memory of his face, all the shock and grief flooded back again. Henny shook herself and blinked her eyes hard. The memory had gone.

"Which way?" she asked briskly, tying her white scarf over the springy red hair that hung down her back in one thick plait. She gazed around at the crowds of townsfolk scurrying so cheerfully about their business. No-one seemed to notice this bewildered family standing in the middle of the street. No-one even paused to look at their drab clothes or at their faces still streaked with mud from the byre where they'd found a warm place to sleep last night, close against a friendly cow.

"Get out o' the road there!" a boy's voice shouted to them urgently from the doorway of a shop. "There's horses comin! Ye'll be run over! Ye'd be safer here with me!"

"Quick!" cried Henny, grabbing little Tam's hand and shepherding all the others over the ruts and puddles to the far side of the road as three heavily laden carts rumbled past. The boy was waiting for them. He seemed to be about eleven or perhaps he was twelve. The same age as Henny herself.

"Ye'll be wantin the mills," said the boy, grinning at her.

His face was very round and a black cap sat jauntily on the back of his head of fair, spiky hair.

"How d'ye ken that?" Henny asked him, her green eyes widening in surprise.

"We get plenty families comin here to the mills, seekin for work. Plenty poor wounded sodgers too, since yon terrible French wars ended. But where's yer faither?"

Henny was silent. Then her mother broke in quietly.

"Deid!" she said. "Drowned at sea three months back. That's why we're here, laddie. Will it matter that there's nae man in the family?"

"Na, it'll help ye!" exclaimed the boy with tactless enthusiasm. "The maister likes to find places for poor widow-women and their bairns whenever he can. They stay on for years and years and they all work hard. They're less fash and bother than men, the maister says. Ye dinna ken onybody at the mills already, do ye? That would help ye fine."

The mother held Davie tighter still.

"My uncle came here with his wife and his young bairns thirty years ago," she said. "But we've heard no word from him in all that time. He might be deid by now."

"Who is he?" asked the boy, his whole face alight with curiosity, his eyes sparkling. "What's his name? If he's still alive, I'm sure to ken him. I ken them all at the mills."

"James Gunn," said the mother, "my faither's youngest brither."

"Jimmy Gunn!" cried the boy. "He's no deid! He's the best overseer in Number One Mill! Jimmy's still a good steady worker though he's weel past sixty. His poor wifie's been deid for years but all his grown-up bairns work with him in the mills. And all his grandchilder too. The maister's sure to tak ye if ye're kin to Jimmy Gunn."

"But where can we find this maister o' yers?" Jockie asked, gazing around at the strange street full of busy people.

"He'll be doun at the mills. He's been showin a few o' his important visitors round the place today. I'm goin back to the mills this minute so ye can all come with me. I only came runnin up here to the Old Toun to get a tool for my faither from our house. My faither's one o' the clockmakers. In fact, he's the best clockmaker in the mills!"

"Do they make clocks at yer mills?" Jockie asked the

14

boy in astonishment, pushing back the dark hair from his forehead. "We thought it was a place for spinnin cotton. That's what we heard at hame in Wick."

The boy laughed.

"It *is* a place for spinnin cotton!" he said. "The clockmakers at our mills have nae spare time for makin clocks. It's their job to mend the spinnin machines – the jeanies and the water-frames and the mules and the injines as we call them. The clockmakers build new injines too, whenever the maister needs them. If ye can mend a clock ye can easy mend a spinnin mule. I can just about mend one mysel. My faither's teachin me."

The family looked at the boy with new respect. He seemed very young to be a mender of broken machines.

"This maister of yours," said the mother, her voice shaking a little. "Is he a good man?"

"Mr Owen? My grannie says he's a wee bit odd in his ideas but he's awful kind. He isna like yon cruel maisters in Dundee or the terrible maisters far awa in England. He never belts or skelps anybody. He never gollers out loud or shouts at us. But he's verra strict. All the hands have to work hard for him in the mills. And ye're no allowed to go drappin bits o' cotton on the floor. Ye have to pick up every wee smitch o' the stuff."

"Hands?" asked Henny, looking down at her own two hands, turning them this way and that. There were freckles on her fingers.

"The hands are the mill-workers," the boy explained with a grin. "I'm a hand mysel. There's almost two thousand hands workin at our mills. Ye'll all be hands too if the maister likes the look o' ye."

"No wee Davie!" exclaimed Jockie indignantly. "He's far too young! He canna talk proper yet!"

"Na, na, no the wean," laughed the boy, looking at the baby in his mother's arms. "And no yer youngest bairns. Mr Owen willna let bairns work in the mills till they're ten years old. They'll come to it later, when they're big enough."

"We'd be glad if ye'd bring us to the mills, laddie," said the mother, lifting Davie to her shoulder with one strong arm and smoothing down her black skirt with the other hand. The baby was wide awake now, smiling around at everyone. "We dinna even ken yer name yet," the mother went on. "We're the Sinclairs from Wick, way up north in Caithness. We're a fishin family – or we used to be a fishin family till my poor man was lost at sea. I'm Christina Sinclair and this tall girl here with the fine red plait is my eldest. She's Henny. Henrietta really, named for her grannie, but we aye just call her Henny. Then there's Jockie. He's eleven, and Betty's eight. Tam's four and this wee babby's called Davie. He's only eighteen months old, poor faitherless bairn."

The boy smiled at them all in turn, nodding his head in greeting.

"I'm Robert Cunningham," he said. "My grannie aye calls me Rab. Ye can call me Rab too, if ye like. Come on. We'll gang down by the pathway through the young trees. It's a bittie rough but we'll get there far quicker that way. The maister's mills are right at the foot o' the glen."

Rab led them off the High Street into a narrow lane

where lines of washing flapped high overhead and a stinking pile of rubbish lay by every doorway. A rat scuttled out in front of them. Betty shrieked.

"I dinna like this place at all, Mammie!" she sobbed, burying her face in her mother's skirt. "I want to gang back hame to Wick! We're too far from the sea here! I canna smell the salt o' the sea any mair! I canna smell the tangle o' seaweed along the sands! We dinna belong here at all!" Betty was small and thin and quick like Jockie, and with the same brown eyes.

"That hungry sea's been too cruel to us, dearie," said her mother, stroking the girl's dark hair. "We're never gangin back to it. I dinna want my Jockie or Tam or wee Davie here to be drowned in the sea like their faither. I dinna want ye two girls made sea-widows, like so many good women at hame in Caithness. Whatever these cotton-mills are like, they canna be as harsh as the sea."

Henny and Jockie hurried to keep up with Rab who was almost running now along a muddy roadway between open green fields. Heavy carts were coming and going close beside them. Carters were swinging their whips and swearing at their horses. In the clear blue sky overhead a buzzard sailed in wide, slow circles, mewing as it flew. Suddenly, Rab turned away from the crowded track and plunged headlong down a steep path between slender trees. The others followed him, their feet slipping and sliding beneath them.

"This must be a forest!" Henny cried in amazement, keeping close to Rab. "I've never seen so many trees! Our hills at hame are almost bare, ye ken. We only have the bracken and the heather up there."

"Look!" Rab said, stopping suddenly and pointing down into the valley.

The whole family stood still. First they saw the sparkling river, far below them, and then they saw the mills. Great long buildings, far grander than churches, six and seven storeys high, built of a darkish pink sandstone, with rows of bright windows shining in the sunlight. Plumes of smoke rose from dozens of chimneys and hung in a thick white haze over the valley. A curious buzz of sound surged up the hill.

"What's that place?" shrieked little Tam, excited and scared at the same time.

"New Lanark!" Rab announced proudly as if he owned the whole village. "Ye can see our four big mills doun there, close by the river. Number One Mill's on the right. The one with the bell-tower on top. That's the place where yer uncle works. Then comes Two and Three. Number Four's on the left. We dinna do any spinnin in Number Four. That's where all the millwrights and the smiths and the clockmakers and the joiners work. My faither's in there. Look, ye can see the maister's grand new Institute right in front. That's a kind o' school. And if ye walk to the back o' the mills near the river ye'll see the sheds where we store the bales o' raw cotton. The bales come here by the cartload, day after day. And look at yon fine rows o' houses where the hands are livin."

"I canna see any houses at all!" said Henny, disappointed, her eyes skimming along the roof of each magnificent building in turn. She was thinking longingly of their own warm little home at Wick, with its hard mud floor and its hearth in the middle of the room. She was remembering how their beloved pigs and hens used to come wandering in and out through the open door all day long and how their cow lay peacefully at night in the byre at one end.

Rab laughed.

"We dinna live in poor wee houses like yon huts ye have up north," he said. "Every family here has a fine room all to itsel. Big families even have two rooms. There's a fire for cookin and there's a table and beds and everythin ye'll ever be wantin. We've got hundreds of folk from Caithness livin doun there. From Thurso mainly."

Christina Sinclair sniffed sharply.

"Thurso's all very weel," she said, "but Wick's far better."

"I could easy drap a stane down yon smoky chimney!" cried Henny. She stooped to pick up a pebble and flung it as hard as she could. It landed harmlessly in a clump of purple foxglove under the trees. A scolding robin hopped away in the grass, startled by the stone.

"It's further than ye think," Rab laughed.

The family slithered and staggered right to the foot of the hill and then onto a bridge over the fast-flowing channel of the mill-lade. Now the huge mills towered high above them like mysterious palaces. The streets were far cleaner here than in the Old Town but the noises were louder. The steady rush of a powerful river sounded from somewhere behind the buildings. From the four tall mills themselves came strange bangings and hammerings and clankings of metal and wood. The whole place was throbbing. The great buildings themselves seemed to vibrate with the terrible racket. Little Davie cried out in fear and clung to his mother's neck.

"Wheesht, Davie laddie!" said Christina, hushing his sobs, but even she looked scared.

"We'll find the maister," said Rab. "Mak sure ye bow or beck when ye meet him. Mr Owen aye likes good manners."

"We dinna ken how to bow or beck!" Henny said indignantly. "We never do that sort o' thing in Wick."

"Then just watch me," said Rab with a laugh. "Ye'll soon learn!"

CHAPTER 2

Kelly's Clock

New Lanark, Scotland, July 1819

"Robert Cunningham!" a man's voice called sharply from close behind Christina Sinclair and her bewildered family. "Where on earth have you been? Your father tells me he sent you up to the Old Town more than an hour ago. He can't get on with his work till you bring him that tool he's waiting for. He's wasting my good time, boy, and so are you!"

"It's the maister!" gasped Rab and spun round to face him. The Sinclairs all turned at the same moment. Rab whipped off his cap and bowed respectfully. Christina did her best to curtsey, juggling the baby on her hip.

The four older children shuffled their dirty bare feet and bent awkwardly at the waist or the knee. Henny gazed up at the man. He seemed to be older than her own father had been. He looked about fifty perhaps. He had large, kind eyes. Soft eyes. A bit like their father's eyes, she thought. That seemed a good sign.

"I'm sorry, sir," said Rab, full of his old perky confidence again. "Ye see, sir, I found these braw folk for ye up in the Old Toun. I ken ye turned awa two families last week because they were no strong enough but this is a really good family, sir. Their name's Sinclair and they come from Wick and their man was lost at sea and Jimmy Gunn's their uncle."

Rab paused to catch his breath again. The master smiled at him and turned to inspect the new family carefully, his large eyes resting on each one in turn.

"Only five children?" he asked at last with a tinge of disappointment in his voice.

"There were three ithers, sir," the mother explained, "but they deed young. These five are all strong and healthy. We ken how to work hard."

"And Jimmy Gunn's your uncle, is he? Jimmy's been here a very long time. He came here back in Mr Dale's day, before I took over the mills. When did you last see him?"

"Thirty years ago, sir. I was only a young lassie then, ye ken, but he's sure to remember me. 'Douce wee Chrissie', he used to call me. My name's Christina, ye see sir." Christina Sinclair gave an embarrassed laugh and rubbed her face.

The master smiled again as he looked at this tall, broad-

22

shouldered woman, Christina Sinclair. She certainly wasn't any longer the sweet little girl her uncle had known in Wick, thirty years ago.

"He's a good man, Jimmy Gunn," said the master, "and his whole family works well for me. Clean, honest and sober, every one of them. Well, my visitors have gone up the river to look at the waterfalls so I'll take you to see Jimmy straight away. If he speaks well of you, I'll let you stay. We've just one house empty since poor old Widow Manson died on Saturday last."

Henny couldn't help noticing the strange lilt of the man's speech. His voice went up and down in a pleasant kind of singsong, very different from the familiar Scots rhythms they were used to. He didn't even sound like an Englishman.

Christina Sinclair curtsied again and moved the baby to her other arm.

"Thank ye, sir," she said.

The master turned to Rab. "Robert Cunningham, you run off now and take that wrench to your father. He's in Number Four. Then come back and find us by Number One. If Jimmy Gunn says a good word for this family, I'll need you to show them to the house."

"Aye, sir," said Rab, bowing quickly again before he ran.

The master led the way towards the mill with the bell-tower on top.

"So you're not a Gaelic speaker, Christina Sinclair?" he asked her as they walked side by side. "We've got hundreds of them here. They come to us from the Highlands and Islands. When I was a young boy in Wales,

23

I used to speak the Welsh language with my grandparents quite a bit, so when I first arrived here at the mills, about twenty years ago, I hoped I might be able to understand these Gaelic speakers but I'm afraid I can't. The Welsh and the Gaelic are not nearly as close as I thought they'd be! After all this time, I still have to get someone to translate the Highlanders into English for me."

"I do speak the Gaelic, sir," Christina said. "It's my mither-tongue and I still speak it at hame sometimes with the bairns but the Gaelic isna so strong in the fishin ports of Caithness as it used to be years ago. We mainly speak the Scots there now."

"Well, Christina Sinclair, I can understand your Scots well enough, thank goodness. You talk plain and clear and slow. That's what I like best. Now here we are at Number One. Wait outside the door and I'll find Jimmy Gunn."

As the master opened the door of the mill, a burst of hot, damp air rushed out into their faces. Their ears were shocked by the deafening clatter and hum of machines. Henny and Jockie leant forward and tried to look inside. They saw high wheels turning, wide belts running, rollers rolling, thousands of spindles spinning, and hundreds of men and women and children, all in bare feet, silently tending those long rows of mysterious machines.

"That isna the way you used to spin the wool at hame, is it, Mammie?" Betty piped up, peering around Henny's arm.

"They must spin differently here, dearie," said her mother, as puzzled as the rest of them. Christina Sinclair hadn't felt so frightened since the terrible night when she'd heard the news that her husband's boat was lost in the storm. Her mouth felt suddenly dry. She stepped quickly back from the mill's noise and the waves of hot air. She drew the children closer to her.

Mr Robert Owen came out through the doorway again with a stooped, grey-haired man at his side.

"Here they are, Jimmy! Your long-lost relations from Wick in Caithness, or so they say. Do you know them?"

The stooped man scratched his head in puzzlement. He pulled on his bushy white beard as his eyes moved slowly from Henny to Jockie and from Betty to Tam.

"Nae, sir. It's thirty years since I left hame, ye ken."

At last he looked at Christina Sinclair herself. She had tears in her eyes as she stepped forward to greet him with Davie still wriggling in her arms.

"Uncle James!" she cried. "Surely you remember me. I'm Christina. Yer brither Alec's lass!"

"It's douce wee Chrissie!" Jimmy Gunn exclaimed in amazement, suddenly recognizing her. "But ye've grown so tall, lassie, and ye've got these five bairns!"

"Aye, and yer dear brither's lang dead, Uncle, and my poor man's lost at sea and we've come here to the mills to find work. Can ye no put in a good word for us?"

"Indeed I can, Chrissie. Maister, I kent this woman when she was only a wee lassie. She comes from a fine family. My own brither's family. She's sure to work hard for ye, sir, and she'll give ye nae trouble at all."

Suddenly Jimmy Gunn rushed towards Christina and hugged her tight, tears in his own eyes now. A fit of

25

coughing seized him. He bent double, gasping for breath. Then he straightened himself slowly as the coughing passed.

"Right!" said Mr Owen, beaming at them all. "That's good enough for me. If you work as well as your uncle here, Christina Sinclair, I'll be well satisfied. Keep your children scrubbed clean and get them to work right on time every morning and tell them I don't allow any fighting or cursing in this village."

"We never curse, sir!" Jockie broke in indignantly, "and we never swear or say bad words. Our mammie willna let us!"

"I'm glad to hear it!" said the master, looking down at Jockie with new interest. Then he turned back to James Gunn.

"Now, Jimmy," he said, "you get back inside your mill again and keep a strict eye on those hands. You'll see this family of yours at the end of the day. Christina Sinclair, you stay here with your children till Robert Cunningham comes to find you. He'll show you the house and tell you where to get your food. You can buy everything on credit for the first month till your wages are paid. The clothes are free. You and the two older children will start work tomorrow morning in Mill Number Two."

With that he was off, striding away to the next mill, humming happily to himself as he went. Suddenly he stopped in his tracks, swung around and came hurrying back again.

"How old's that boy?" he asked, pointing at Jockie.

"Eleven last birthday, sir," said his mother.

26

"Can he read?"

"Aye, he can read a bit, sir, though he was only two years in the school. He's never tried the writin yet."

"Just as well!" exclaimed Mr Owen sharply. "These children of yours get pushed into reading and writing far too young, before they can understand a word of it! I suppose they made you read the Bible and the Church Catechism at your school, boy, did they?"

"They did, sir," said Jockie, quite proud of himself.

"Do you understand those books?"

"Nae sir. I can just say the words out loud. They're too hard to understand. Mammie says I'll understand them fine when I'm older."

"Just as I thought!" said the master with a deep sigh. "It's a sad waste of time, all that foolish Bible reading, all that learning of questions and answers about religion! If you want to read something, boy, *Robinson Crusoe*'s the only book you'll ever need. When I was a lad your age, I read it over and over again. That's the book to teach you how to live! Now, what do you really know, boy? Tell me something you've found out for yourself. Something you've seen with your own two eyes. Not something you've read in the Bible."

"I ken a lot about fishin boats, sir," said Jockie, grinning happily up at Mr Owen. "I can easy tell whose boats are comin into the harbour at Wick just by lookin at the riggin o' their sails. And I ken a lot about birds, sir. Sea birds and river birds. I ken all their names and their different cries and where to find their nests and what colour their eggs are and when they'll fly awa to a

27

different country and when they'll fly back again."

"Well done, boy!" exclaimed the master, rubbing his hands together and smiling his approval. "It's a hundred times better to know about ships and birds than to be spouting a catechism that was never meant for children! You seem a sensible lad and you've got a good tongue in your head. We could do with a boy like you up at our house. Braxfield House. The last lad was no good at all. He kept on stealing things. I tried talking kindly to him but he went on stealing and in the end he had to go. What we need is someone to clean the shoes and bring in the coal and carry out the ashes and do all the odd jobs about the place. How would you like that, boy? Sheddon would train you well."

"Is yer house far awa, sir?" asked Jockie, his dark eyes apprehensive.

"No, no! Not far. Just a short walk from here. Less than a mile. You'd have to sleep at Braxfield House, of course, up in the servants' attic, but you could come back to see your mother here in the village every Sunday afternoon."

"I thought I'd be workin on the big machines," said Jockie. He sounded disappointed.

"I don't want to force you, boy. Start in the mills with your mother and your sister tomorrow morning if that's what you want. After a week or so, I'll talk to you again. A place in my house would give you a far better start in life. You might even grow up to be a fine butler, like Sheddon himself. Think about it!"

Jockie nodded. Mr Owen turned back to the mother.

"Don't forget, Christina Sinclair, you'll be at work with

the older girl and the boy at six in the morning," said the master. "That baby can go straight to the nursery and the two younger children can play outside till school starts at half past seven. Don't be late, any of you! Not even one minute late! And wash yourselves all over before you go to bed tonight! Is that clear?"

Christina Sinclair nodded.

"We'll all be clean, sir," she murmured.

Mr Owen was satisfied. He left them with a wave of his hand just as Robert Cunningham came running back.

"First, I'll show ye the clock!" Rab panted, almost out of breath. "The maister likes everybody to see it. 'Kelly's clock' we still call it, though the man that made it left our mills a few years back. The maister says Kelly's clock is the beatin heart o' New Lanark. The river drives the clock and the mills all at the same time."

"What's a clock?" asked Tam, tugging on Rab's arm.

"It's a wee machine for tellin the time, Tam. Ye probably never needed one up in Caithness but ye'll need it here. Come on. Kelly's famous clock is just inside Number One Mill."

The whole family trooped through the doorway after Rab. Their ears were battered by the violent noise of machines. Their skin began to sweat in the hot, damp air. Rab was pointing excitedly to a strange contraption fixed to the wall. Henny saw a large round ring, a circle almost like a face. Inside the face she saw four smaller rings. Mysterious numbers were written around the edge of every face.

"We call these five rings the dials," Rab shouted over

the din. "This big dial has three hands, ye see. One long hand points to the seconds, sixty in every minute. The other long hand shows the minutes and the wee hand shows the hours. Now look at these four smaller dials. The one on the left tells ye the days o' the week – like Monday, Tuesday, Wednesday. There's nae Sunday marked here because we dinna work on Sundays. That's the day of rest, ye ken. The dial up at the top shows ye the weeks in each month and the dial on the right gives ye the months of the year. This dial at the bottom tells ye the years. It gangs up to ten years and then it starts again."

"But who bothers to look at a clock?" asked Henny in amazement, gazing up at the five round faces on the wall. The dials seemed to stare back at her without a smile.

"Everyone at these mills needs a clock!" said Rab. "Whenever we look at these dials we know what time o' day it is and what day o' the week it is and what month o' the year it is and how many years we've worked at the mill. The bell-ringer aye keeps his eye on the biggest dial so he kens exactly when to ring the bell for workin and restin and school and sleepin. Strict time-keepin! That's what the maister wants in his mills."

"But ye could just look up at the sun!" protested Jockie. "When the sun rises, ye jump out o' yer bed. When the sun's overhead, ye eat yer dinner. When the sun sets, ye gang back to yer bed. That's what we did at hame by the sea."

"The mill's different," explained Rab seriously. "It runs like clockwork and all the mill-hands run by clockwork too. The poor old sun's nae use to us. The sun gets up early in summer and late in winter but we must work the same hours, winter and summer. We're tied to Kelly's clock, ye see. It's the only proper way to run a spinnin mill, the maister says."

Christina shook her head in bewilderment. She'd never thought of a day being divided up into hours and minutes and seconds in that odd way. She'd always counted the past in sharp memories, not in years.

"Ye'll soon get the hang of it," laughed Rab. "Now I'll tak ye downstairs to see the great water-wheel. The maister aye likes new folk to look at the wheel. He wants his hands to understand how the mill works. He says they'll work much better if they understand."

Down in the basement, the Sinclair family stared up at an enormous wheel, slowly turning and turning in a steady stream of water that fell onto it from the lade above. The air smelt damp. Water dripped and trickled quietly. The wheel hissed.

"It's no goin verra fast," said Jockie, disappointed.

"Fast enough," said Rab. "That big wheel turns a smaller one, geared into its rim, up there, see. Then the smaller one turns one smaller still and so on. The smaller the wheel, the faster it turns. Then the power's taken up from the fastest wheel by belts and pulleys to drive the injines on every floor of the mill. D'ye follow what I'm sayin?"

The family laughed with one voice.

"Na!" said Henny. "Maybe one day we'll understand!"

Rab laughed with them. He led them upstairs and outside into the open air again.

"We'll gang to Widow Manson's house in Caithness Row," he said. "She lived there for twenty years and the place was in an awful state on the day she deed. I saw it mysel. But now it's been all redd up and made clean by the neighbour women. Most o' the folk in Caithness Row come from yer ain country in the north, so ye'll soon feel at hame. Pick up yer sacks now."

Henny and Jockie, Betty and Tam stooped to take up the bundles they'd let drop to the ground. As the whole family followed Rab away from the grinding clamour of the four high mills, their ears caught again the steady pulsing sound of water. Rushing, bubbling, laughing, tumbling water, hidden away somewhere, just out of their sight.

"That's our great river ye can hear," Rab said proudly. "The River Clyde, on the far side of our mills. Some o' the river-water comes doun a tunnel and flows through the lade here and turns the big wheels in the mills like the one I showed ye. Then it falls back into the river again. We've had a wet summer this year so the Clyde's full and fast. Lucky it's nae too full. If it's too full or too low, we have awful trouble with our big water-wheels. I'll tak ye to see the river soon. We swim there on hot days if the water's low and we lowp from rock to rock."

Christina Sinclair froze.

"Nae, my bairns!" she cried, fear rising in her voice. "Dinna ye gang anywhere near yon river! We've had our fill o' sorrow from the water o' the sea. Enough sorrow to last us a lifetime. So keep well awa from the water o' the river. D'ye hear me?"

"Aye, Mammie," the four of them chorused politely. Even little Davie seemed to be nodding his head in solemn agreement.

But as Rab led the whole family out of the daylight and into the third stairway along Caithness Row, he turned to give Henny a quick, sly wink. Henny winked back at him, her green eyes sparkling with sudden, wild excitement. Whatever her mother might say about the terrible dangers of water, Henny wanted to see that powerful river as soon as she could.

CHAPTER 3

A Room in the Sky

New Lanark, July 1819

At the top of the stairs, Rab turned left and pushed open a door. The Sinclair family followed him into a square room, lit by high windows. The walls were bright with fresh whitewash. The floorboards were newly scrubbed. Christina let out a cry of pleasure and surprise. She lowered Davie to the floor and let him stagger about by himself from table to chair. There was no fire burning in the iron grate but Widow Manson's old black pot and kettle still hung there from the swee, reminding them of the things they'd had to leave at home.

"Where are the beds?" asked Betty, looking around the room. She could see no springy mattresses of heather lying on the floor like the ones at their old house in Wick.

"Here!" Rab cried in triumph, whipping back first one curtain and then another to reveal two beds tucked right into the wall. Then he bent down and pulled out two more beds from underneath, each one trundling over the floor on squeaky wooden wheels.

"Folk round here call these the hurlie-beds," he said. "There's plenty room. Only two to a bed and one bed left empty. Or yer mother and Jockie could each have a bed to theirsels, though it's never so warm to sleep all on yer lane!"

Betty and Tam had climbed onto one of the hurlie-beds and were jumping noisily up and down on the straw mattress.

"Wheesht!" said their mother, her finger on her lips. The two of them stopped their racket at once and lay flat on their backs, side by side on the bed, pretending to be good.

Meanwhile, Jockie was inspecting a round white chamber-pot in one corner of the room.

"What's this thing, Rab?" he asked, pushing it gently with his foot.

"That's the chantie," Rab laughed. "There's aye a chantie for every house. Ye can easy guess what it's for! Ye have to be sure to tip it out every day in one o' the privies in yon row o' wee huts out the back. Every privy's got a fine wee seat on top and a big tin can underneath. The 'necessary', some folks call the privy. Yon chantie saves ye from goin all the way doun the stairs to the necessary in the middle of the night!"

The children stared at Rab in amazement. These arrangements seemed so much more complicated than the simple hole in the heather that they'd used at home.

"And I'll tell ye somethin else ye must do," Rab went on. "Ye must put any rubbage on the midden heap doun in the street. Potato peelins and tea leaves and wee scraps o' this and that. Then in the mirk night, when ye're fast asleep, the scavengers come and they sweep up the middens and they tak the stuff awa on their cart. They tak awa the privy cans too and put in the clean ones! That's a job I'll never be wantin! The scavengers spread all the muck on the farmers' fields. The farmers say it's good manure for their crops but it maks an awful stink on the farms by the Clyde at this time o' year."

Rab held his nose and grinned at their surprised faces.

Christina Sinclair was not really listening to Rab. She was busy lifting the lid of the low kist under the window where warm, white blankets were stored. She was running her hands over the wooden bink or dresser against the wall, with its wash-basin and jug, its neat rows of cups and plates, and then she was gently touching the solid table near the fireplace, with its four chairs and its low stools or creepies for the children.

"He's thought of everythin, this maister o' yers!" she said, turning to Rab in admiration.

"That's just what my grannie aye says about the maister!" cried Rab with a laugh. "She thinks he's great. But my faither isna so pleased with it at all. He says the mill-workers should learn to stand on their ain feet.

That's why he'll no live down here in the village though he works for Mr Owen at the mills. He says he feels free, livin up in the Old Toun where the maister canna rule his whole life from mornin to sky-settin. He reckons the hands in New Lanark'll soon be nae better than yon poor black slaves over the sea in Carolina. Everythin's been done for them for years so now they've gone far too quiet. 'Sheep-like', my faither calls them. And he says they're like the silly coos in the byre, waitin to be milked. They'll no stand up for theirsels, my faither says."

"What does your mither think?" asked Christina, smiling down at him.

Rab took a while to answer. His voice was sad.

"My minnie died when I was born. My grannie's the only minnie I have now. She's aye good to me."

"But why does yer faither no just leave the mills and go back to his clockmakin if he's no wantin to be like a slave in Carolina?" Henny asked him, pushing quickly away from her mind the terrible news that Rab's mother was dead. It hurt her even to think of it. "Yer faither'd feel really free then. He'd be his own maister."

"But, Henny, he maks a good steady livin for hissel down here at the mills," said Rab. "There's work every day and a sure wage at the end of every month. Clockmakin's far more mischancie, he says. Onyways, Grannie thinks it's better for him to work for the maister and he aye likes to please my grannie."

"Yer grannie sounds a verra sensible woman!" said Christina Sinclair firmly, unwrapping the bundles from home and putting away their precious bits and pieces in the kist.

"We'll just leave the Book here," she said, placing her black Bible carefully on the table. "Jockie, ye can be readin us a portion the night, just before we sleep. Yer faither would be wantin that. I wasna very happy about those hard words Mr Owen had for the Bible and the catechism. I canna read a word o' them mysel, it's true, but I'll mak sure ye bairns can read them loud and clear."

Rab laughed.

"That's what all the folk from Caithness say and all the Highlanders too!" he said. "They think the maister's ideas about the Bible are awful shockin. But they're glad to work for him all the same and he aye lets the Highlanders have their Gaelic chapel in the New Buildings every sabbath. Ye can gang there yersels if yer wantin the Gaelic service or ye can have a different kind o' chapel in the Big Hall in the Institute or ye can gang up to the kirk in the Old Toun. There's a thousand folk go walkin up there to Lanark every single Sabbath to hear the minister. My grannie says Mr Menzies is a grand preacher but the maister disna like Mr Menzies and Mr Menzies disna like him! The maister thinks the mill folk are daft to keep to the kirk, but he lets them be."

At the end of the afternoon, after Rab had helped the family to buy oatmeal, bread, meat, milk, tea and sugar at the village store, he led them to the room where they had to collect their free clothing. Each one of them, even Davie, pulled strange garments off the pile of new clothes and held them up with shouts of laughter.

"Try this one on, Jockie," Rab said. "Pull off yer breeks."

Jockie pulled off his trousers and jacket. He stuck his head inside the short cotton tunic that Rab was holding out to him. He pushed his arms into the sleeves. Christina stared at her son in horror.

"Ye canna wear that daft wee thing, Jockie lad!" she said. "It maks ye look like a lassie!"

Rab laughed.

"That's what all the new folk say when they see the clothes at first," he said. "But the maister says ye must all wear the tunics for yer work. Short for the lads, longer for the lassies and down to the ankles for the women. Ye'll get three sets each and ye'll change them three times a week."

"Three times!" Christina gasped.

"But Rab, where's yer ain wee tunic?" said Henny suddenly, looking at his clothes. "Did the maister say ye could wear yer breeks?"

Rab's face flushed with embarrassment.

"Na. I wear my tunic doun here in the mills like all the ither lads," he said. "But I dinna wear it up in Old Lanark. All the folk up there laugh at me in the street if they see me wearin yon tunic. They call me 'lassie', ye ken, and 'mill-bairn'. So I wear my own breeks up in the town. I was up there earlier, ye ken, and then I just kept my breeks on all the day. The maister didna say a word."

"But why does the maister want the lads to wear yon funny wee kilties?" Henny asked him.

"He says they're hailsome," Rab explained. "And he says the Roman soldiers wore just the same thing in the old days."

Christina shook her head in bewilderment.

"Roman soldiers!" she murmured under her breath.

As soon as the new food had been stowed away in the cupboard under the dresser and the new clothes folded into the kist, Rab took the family along to their uncle's house in Long Row. They walked into a room just like their own, at the top of a stair, and full of cousins they had never met before. Uncle James's grown-up sons and daughters were there to welcome them and so were all his grandchildren, a few of them only babies like Davie, but others as old as Henny and Jockie and already working in the mills.

"We're a true mill family and verra proud of it!" said Uncle James, choking back his cough and beaming around at everyone as his eldest married daughter dished up the supper. "But tell me now, Chrissie lass, what's been happenin up there in Caithness in all these years since I left the dear old place? Do ye still see yon thick white haar hangin over the sea in the early mornins? And how's the fishin and how are the good old friends and all the weel-kent families in Wick?"

Christina had so much to tell him. Stories of good times and bad times, of grand catches of silver herrings, thrashing about in the nets; of wild storms and boats lost at sea with all the fishermen drowned; of births, marriages and deaths; of the many poor folk who had packed up and sailed away to Canada to find a new life. Uncle James listened intently to every word she said, nodding his head, wiping his eyes, laughing out loud, coughing again. His grandchildren were restless. They had never been to that distant country of Caithness, still so vivid in his memory. They wanted to tell the new family all about the mill and the village and the river and about the great annual Lanimer Day up in the Old Town.

"Ye've missed Lanimers this year," one of the older girl cousins whispered excitedly to Henny. "It aye comes late in May or early June. Next year we'll tak ye walkin round the big stanes that mark the edges of Lanark. There's drums and processions and singin and dancin in the streets. The men aye have a few drams o' whisky."

"What does the maister say?" Henny asked her in surprise.

"He disna like it!" the cousin laughed. "Too much noise and drinkin, he says. But he canna stop it. He's tried hard enough but in the end he had to give us a holiday for Lanimers, just like New Year's Day."

Jockie had a quite different problem of his own to ask this cousin about.

"How can ye wake up in time for the mills in the mornins?" he said with a puzzled frown.

"The bells wake us!" the cousin explained. "When the first bell starts to tingle, we all lowp out of bed and wash our faces and pull on our clothes. On the next bell, we run doun the stairs in a great rush and we hurry to the mills. The maister says we must be inside the mill door before yon bell stops its ringin at exactly six o'clock."

"But dinna ye stop to eat somethin first?" asked Henny.

"Na, we eat later," said the cousin. "We stop for breakfast at nine and there's anither break for dinner at two. We finish for the day at half past six and then we eat

41

our supper and go to the school."

"School at night!" protested Jockie in horror.

All the cousins nodded solemnly.

"I can read a bit already," Jockie boasted, rather too pleased with himself. "I'll no bother goin to the school."

"It isna just the readin we learn at the night-school," said another cousin. "There's singin and dancin and geography and wild animals and everythin."

"Wild animals!" Jockie shouted, leaping up from his stool in excitement. "I want to see them! Where does the maister keep them?"

The cousins laughed.

"There's nae real wild animals," one of the older boys explained. "Just big pictures of lions and tigers and elephants and giraffes hangin up on the walls in our Institute. They're the only animals allowed in New Lanark. The maister'll no let us keep pigs or dogs or hens in our houses. He thinks animals are a wee bit too clarty and dirty to live inside the houses with us."

Henny gasped at such an odd idea.

"But surely some folk try to smuggle in a pig," she said.

The cousins looked shocked.

"The maister'd be sure to find out," said the older boy seriously. "Then there'd be trouble."

"But he looks such a kind man," said Henny. "His eyes are soft and gentle. A bit like our faither."

"Aye, he's kind," said the boy. "But he's verra strict as weel."

Two hours later, the Sinclairs were back in their own room and all tucked up in the soft, warm beds. Henny lay awake for a while with little Davie curled close beside her, his thumb comfortably in his mouth. She looked around at this strange new home. Her mother had left the shutters wide open and the white moonlight was streaming in through the windows. She only wished that her father could be there to see it all. He would have been amazed at a room like this, so high up in the sky. He would have been astonished to see his family living in a mill-village, so far from the sea. She could imagine his kind, brown eyes opening wide in surprise as he stepped in through that doorway. She knew how he'd smile to see his wife and children in their fine new beds. As she drifted off to sleep, Henny heard an owl hooting softly in the distance, and all through her dreams she heard the rush and swirl of the river.

CHAPTER 4

A Wee Block of Wood

New Lanark, July 1819

The first morning bell was ringing! Startled, the whole Sinclair family leapt out of bed. They washed their faces in cold water and pulled on their cotton clothes, laughing out loud at how strange they looked in this new mill-uniform. Christina lifted Davie up in her arms. She opened the door.

"Which way?" Betty asked as the Sinclairs joined all the other families who were pounding down the stairs in bare feet, smoothing their hair with damp fingers and chattering happily with each other as they ran. The second bell started to ring.

"Are ye new?" a pleasant-faced boy asked Betty, overhearing her question. He was about the same age as Henny. He held the hand of a tiny child who jumped carefully from step to step.

Betty nodded.

"We dinna ken which way to go," she said.

"I'll show ye!" said the boy proudly. "I'm Ian McGregor. I was born here so I ken everythin! We have to leave our weans at the nursery first. That babby in yer mammie's arms can go there. The nursery's on the ground floor of the maister's grand new Institute. I'm takin my brither there before I start work, so I'll easy show ye the way. Ye can play outside at peevers or spinnin yer peerie till it's time for lessons to begin."

Betty skipped along happily beside the boy, listening to all his explanations. The rest of her family trailed slowly behind her, not quite so eager for the day to begin as she was.

"That wee lassie o' mine meets every new mornin and every new stranger with a trustin smile," her mother murmured quietly to Henny, shaking her head a little, almost as if Betty's friendliness was something to be worried about.

The Institute for the Formation of Character was a tall, stone building with long windows. Out in front was a fenced playground full of children, all of them dressed in the same short tunics of plain cotton cloth and all playing together in the bright morning sunshine. Hoops were rolling, tops were spinning. Girls were skipping with ropes or hopping from one chalked square to the next. Boys were leaping over each other's backs or flicking marbles into a ring. The whole playground was ringing with children's shouting and laughter.

"There's Molly Young," said Ian McGregor, pointing to a plump, kind-looking girl of about seventeen who was hurrying towards them. "She looks after the weans. They just play games all day long and listen to stories and sing songs. They can lie down and have a sleep whenever they want. Yer babby'll be fine with Molly."

Reluctantly, Christina Sinclair placed Davie into Molly's outstretched arms. Davie let out a bellow of rage.

"A new wee boy!" cried Molly in delight. "I'll tak good care of him. What's his name?"

"Davie," said Christina, still clutching her baby's hand, not wanting to let him go.

"Hush now, Davie," said Molly, stroking his warm, pink cheek. "I'll be tellin ye a fine story soon." Davie stopped crying and looked up at Molly with a surprised smile. She turned back to his mother. "And how many bairns for the school?"

"There's Betty here," said Christina. "She's eight. And Tam's four."

"Betty will be in one of the schoolrooms upstairs. There's rows and rows o' desks there, Betty. Ye're sure to love it. And Tam will go with Mr Buchanan into the infants' room. Mr Buchanan'll be teaching ye all his funny poems, Tam, about the sheep and the cows. He'll tak ye walking under the trees to see the birds and the

46

flowers. Ye'll have a fine time with Mr Buchanan. Run in there now, Tam, and give him yer name. Then ye can come out here and play."

Molly pointed the way and Tam scampered off on his thin little legs towards the open door. He seemed full of new confidence. Betty rushed to join a group of girls who were taking turns to skip over a long, turning rope.

Christina was bewildered at having to part so suddenly with her three youngest children like this. When she'd worked at cleaning and packing the herring by the harbour in Wick, the children had always played close beside her the whole day long. She felt lost without them.

"I want to see the wild animals!" Jockie whispered urgently to Ian. The great bell was still ringing, on and on.

"Quick, then!" said the boy, eager to help. "We've only got a minute. We'll dash upstairs before the bell stops and ye'll see the wild animals. Bring yer big sister too."

Henny and Jockie ran up the stairs with Ian and into a vast hall. There, hanging high on the walls, were large coloured pictures of very strange animals. Ian pointed to each one in turn and recited their names. Elephant and tiger, lion and bear, giraffe and rhinoceros. Henny and Jockie tipped back their heads and stared. They had never even heard of such animals before.

"I wish they were real," breathed Henny. "Then I could play with them!"

"Do they all bark like dogs?" Jockie asked seriously. Ian just laughed. "Quick!" he said. "We'll find yer mammie again and I'll tak ye to the door of Number Two Mill. That's aye the place for new folk. Yon bell'll be stoppin soon. We canna be late."

When they arrived, breathless, at Number Two Mill, Ian suddenly waved goodbye to them and leapt in through the open doorway. At that very moment, the bell stopped ringing. The village street was strangely quiet and empty. The mills and the schools seemed to have swallowed up the whole population. Then one solitary girl, limping badly, panting and gasping to catch her breath, came hobbling up to the door.

"Grizzie, ye're late again!" shouted a stern voice from within.

"Sorry, sir," came the girl's soft voice. "I just couldna wake up."

"Get along to yer work, then, and set yer monitor to black. If the maister asks ye why, tell him ye were one minute late."

"Aye, sir," said the girl sadly. She limped into the mill and disappeared from sight.

Henny looked at Jockie. Their mother looked at each of them in turn.

"We'll no be likin this place," Henny whispered.

"Can we no gang back hame to the sea, Mammie?" asked Jockie.

Their mother shook her head.

"Be brave," she said simply. "That's what yer dear faither would be wantin."

At that moment a cheery, red-faced man with a short black beard bustled out of the mill to greet them.

"Ah, the new family from Wick," he said, running his eyes critically over each one in turn. "The maister told me ye'd be here. Kin to Jimmy Gunn from Number One Mill, is that right? I'm Willie Grant, first overseer for this mill. Tell me yer names."

"I'm Christina Sinclair," said the mother. "Henny's twelve and Jockie's eleven. The maister asked Jockie to work for him up at Braxfield House but the laddie wants to try the mill first."

Willie Grant looked down at Jockie in surprise.

"Ye'd be far better off at the maister's fine house, Jockie," he said. "It's cleaner and quieter up there and the work's no heavy. But the maister'll want ye to choose for yersel, lad. That's aye his way. Come awa in, the three o' ye!"

Willie Grant stepped into his mill. Christina followed with Henny and Jockie close behind her. At once Henny clapped her hands over her ears. The spinning machines pounded and rattled and banged. Willie Grant led them past long rows of clanking wheels and ranks of whirling spindles. Overhead, black leather belts were running down to the machines and up again. The air in the mill was warm and damp, full of wisps of white fluff. Bright morning sunlight flooded in through the high windows, lighting up great clouds of cotton dust. The fluff caught in the back of Henny's throat and she started to cough.

"Those wee scraps o' cotton are just the flue as we call it here," the overseer shouted cheerfully to Henny over the noise. "It's sure to make ye cough a bit at first and it'll stick in yer hair, but ye'll soon get used to it." Henny thought of Uncle James's terrible cough. He didn't seem to have got used to the cotton flue, not in all his long

49

years at New Lanark.

Willie Grant stopped suddenly near a young boy who was down on his hands and knees on the oily floor, ready to crawl right under one of the machines. He had a small brush in one hand and a dust-pan in the other. The overseer turned to Jockie and raised his voice again to make sure he was heard.

"Now lad, ye'll start off learnin how to sweep up the cotton flue under these water-frames with Donny here. Ye're still small enough to creep underneath. Mind ye watch Donny and do just what he tells ye. Ye must never touch the movin belts. Dinna stick yer hand into the machine or ye'll lose it! Donny'll show ye the way. If ye get on well as a sweeper, I'll promote ye to oilin the spindles in a few weeks. That's if ye decide to stay in the mill. All right?"

Jockie looked terrified but he nodded.

"Doun ye go then," said Willie Grant. "Here's a pan and brush. Donny MacInnes, ye're to look after this new lad and teach him the job."

"Aye, sir," murmured the boy as he began to edge forwards, flat on his stomach. His bare legs were already smeared with black oil from the slippery floor.

Jockie dropped to the floor and followed the boy. Christina had one hand to her mouth in horror as she watched him disappearing underneath the throbbing monster. She felt sure she would never see her son again.

"He'll be fine," the overseer called out to her reassuringly, laughing at her alarm. "Donny'll keep a good eye on him. Donny's trained plenty o' young lads in this mill and they've come to nae harm at all. Dinna ye worry about Jockie's fine new clothes gettin in a mess under there. Ye'll change them three times a week, ye ken, and scrub the dirty ones clean. Bare feet in the mill, winter and summer. If ye've got any shoes, just keep them for the Sabbath when ye walk up the hill to the fine kirk in Lanark."

Willie Grant hurried on with Christina on one side and Henny on the other. Henny kept glancing back to watch Jockie under the machine.

"Now, Christina," the overseer shouted, smiling at her cheerfully. "I'm goin to set ye to learn the spinnin on these water-frames. That's the main work in this mill, ye ken. Drawin, twistin, spinnin and windin. In Number Three, where we keep the hand mules, most o' the spinners are men. It's heavy work, turning yon wheels. But here on the water spindles, the women can manage easy."

"I thought the machines did the work," said Christina in surprise.

"Aye, they do. The water power turns eleven thousand spindles in this mill but ye'll have to watch yer machine like a hawk. Ye have to keep one eye on the weighted rollers up there to see they keep turning smoothly, and another eye on the row of spindles down here and on all these hundreds o' threads as they're drawn out thin and twisted. It's the twist that makes them strong enough for the weavin, ye ken. Then the machine winds the threads from the spindles into cops on the bobbins, so ye must watch the bobbins too. When the cop's full, ye take off the bobbin and put on a new one. From time to time ye'll have to take yer turn round the back of the machine, makin sure that the rovins o' cotton are fed nice and steady into the rollers. D'ye follow all that?"

Christina shook her head. There were tears in her eyes.

The overseer laughed. He simply shouted more loudly still.

"Ye'll soon get the knack, Christina Sinclair. Just stand beside Mary Swanson here. She's been spinnin on this fine machine for years. Mary's from Caithness, just like yersel."

Christina took her stand beside Mary Swanson, her pale face turned towards the whirling spindles and the chattering bobbins. She only wished she were holding a cold, slippery herring in one hand and a good sharp knife in the other. Gutting fish by the edge of the sea was work she knew how to do.

"Just watch me this mornin," Mary Swanson bellowed over the noise with a friendly grin. "Ye dinna have to do anythin yet but keep yer eyes on my hands and see what I'm doin. I'll be watching yon threads as they spin and I'll be takin off the full bobbins and checkin on the rovins round the back and callin up the young piecers when we need them to mend our broken threads."

Christina stared at the machine in astonishment as it clanked and shuddered. She watched intently as the water-frame drew out the long threads from between the black rollers, twisting each one with a flick from the sharp point at the tip of the spindle till the strands locked firmly together. Then she saw how the new threads were wound onto the bobbins, each one building up into a beautifully shaped cop or cone. Within a few minutes, Christina's head was reeling dizzily, her eyes were aching, her throat was parched, her ears were bombarded with the frightening noise.

"I'll never get used to it!" she gasped, clutching at Mary Swanson's arm to steady herself.

Mary laughed comfortably.

"Aye, ye will, Christina!" she shouted. "Everybody finds this work awful hard at first but soon it'll seem as easy as handlin yon silvery herrin at hame by the sea. Before long, ye'll be spinnin in yer sleep almost! The machine gives ye the rhythm, regular as clockwork, and ye just work in time with the machine. Ye dinna even have to think."

Christina blinked her eyes in disbelief. Suddenly she noticed a small girl standing close beside her. The girl couldn't have been a day more than ten years old. She seemed much younger than Jockie.

"Are ye doin the spinnin too, lassie?" Christina asked, bending down to speak right into the girl's ear.

"Na!" the girl called back to her. "I'm one o' the piecers. I join up the threads when they break."

"How?" Christina asked in amazement.

"Like this!" said the girl, taking two ends of a broken thread and rolling them deftly between her fingers. In some miraculous way, the thread was perfect again.

"Ye seem awful small to be piecin in a mill, lassie," Christina said to her. "Do ye like the work?"

"I'm a wee bit small but I'm as strong as a horse," the

girl said proudly. "The only hard thing is that we canna sit doun. I must keep on my feet all day long. I'm glad when the break comes for breakfast and dinner. Then I can run hame for a while. I eat somethin and I lie on the bed till my poor legs stop stangin."

Now, at last, Willie Grant turned to Henny.

"Ah!" he said, "The lassie wi the red hair. What's yer name, again? I've forgotten it."

"Henny," she said.

"Right, Henny, I'm takin ye up to the top floor o' this grand mill o' mine. That's where we split open the big bales of cotton that come over the sea in ships from Carolina and other faraway places. First we do the scutchin to get rid of any seeds and dirt from the raw cotton, and then we spread it out into a nice flat lap before we feed it into one o' the cardin engines. We've got whole rows o' splendid cardin engines up there. Best in the whole world! Every one as big as an elephant! Well, near as big as an elephant. The cardin engines straighten out the fibres and bind them into long soft ropes that we call the slivers. Then the drawin machine pulls the slivers into thinner ropes that we call the rovins, ready to be spun on the water-frames. Is that clear?"

"Na!" cried Henny, utterly bewildered by all the overseer's talk about scutching and carding and laps and slivers and rovings. It was a whole new language.

He smiled patiently down at her.

"I'll find some kind lassie yer own age to teach ye, Henny. It's a happy place up there on the top floor. Lots o' fine folk from Caithness, just like yersel. And good folk from the Isle of Skye. Always singin the old sea-songs, they are! Ye can make a start on the scutchin, Henny. That's an easy job. I'll move ye onto the harder work when ye're more used to the place."

Henny trudged up the stone stairs behind Willie Grant. In a long room at the top of the mill, the air was thick with fluff as the raw cotton spilled out of its bales and was pulled this way and that by dozens of deft hands. The overseer set Henny to work beside Effie MacQueen, a girl not much older than herself.

"D'ye speak the Gaelic?" Effie demanded, with a touch of suspicion in her voice.

"A wee bit," said Henny.

The girl smiled at her.

"And the Scots language as weel?"

Henny nodded more confidently.

"Good. Ye'll fit in fine in this mill. Now, watch me and copy me!"

Henny's hands were shaking nervously as she plunged them into the soft creamy cotton and pulled out a huge bundle of the stuff. She picked at the prickly seeds and twigs and shook out the red foreign dust. When the bell for breakfast rang at nine o'clock her wrists and fingers were aching and weary. Work stopped at once. The machines were halted. Henny ran down the stairs with Effie MacQueen and followed her along the street in a broad tide of chattering workers, all on their way home for breakfast. In the Sinclair family's room in Caithness Row, Christina dished up the porridge that had been cooking gently all night long in the black pot. Everyone talked at once. There was so much to say.

"We did our readin and writin at the long desks," explained Betty, bursting with excitement, "and then the desks were whisked up to the ceilin on pulleys."

"Why?" asked her mother in amazement.

"We'll be havin marchin and dancin next," she said. "And after dinner the dominie'll let down all the wild animals and we'll learn about the countries where they live."

Christina shook her head in amazement. "Dancin! In the school! I'm sure the bairns never did dancin in the school at Wick," she said. "It disna seem quite proper! What would the minister say?"

All too soon, the bell rang out for the end of the break. Work was about to start again. Henny was thankful to find Effie MacQueen in the crowd as the families flowed back to the mills and the schools.

"Hurry, Henny!" cried Effie, urging her up the stairs of Number Two. "This is the time when the overseer comes round to check our monitors. Mine's showin white today and I'm wantin to see the smile on his face. Ye'll soon have a monitor yersel."

"What is it?" Henny asked, puzzled. "Is it a person?"

"Na! It's only a wee block o' wood. Did ye no see them? They're the maister's brilliant idea. He calls them his 'silent monitors'. Every one o' the mill-hands has a wee block o' wood hangin up by her own workplace. The four sides are painted white, yella, blae, and black. If ye work weel all day long, and ye're clean and tidy, and if ye dinna come late and ye dinna give any cheek to the overseer, the next mornin yer monitor's turned to white. If ye were quite good but no perfit, it's yella. If ye mak lots o' mistakes and waste yer time then it's blae. Worst of all, when ye come late in the mornin or yer work's awful bad or ye swear or mess about or try stealin a cop o' cotton, then yer monitor's turned to black."

"Do ye get a beatin if it's black?" Henny gasped in terror.

"Na, na, naethin like that!" laughed Effie. "The overseer just looks at yer monitor and then he looks at ye. Everyone all around ye looks at it too. They stare! Sometimes even the maister hissel comes round and he looks at yer monitor and then he looks straight into yer eyes. A pityin sort o' look he gives ye and he shakes his head so sadly. Ye feel terrible bad if yer monitor's black or even if it's blae."

"I wouldna care!" said Henny boldly. "A wee block o' wood canna hurt me! I dinna mind who sees it!"

"Ye will soon mind!" laughed Effie. "Ye'll be thinkin of naethin else when ye've been workin here for a few weeks. If the maister looks at ye with those big kind eyes of his, ye'll be wantin to vanish through the floor. Ye'll be longin to have the white side showin next day. Ye'll be wantin to mak the maister smile at ye again."

Henny shivered suddenly though the weather was warm and the mill was hot. She sank her fingers into the cotton and kept working away steadily at the scutching until the next break. After dinner back with her family, the long afternoon's work dragged slowly on till half past six. She wondered what the mills would be like in winter when the days were short and dark. At least in summer they were flooded with light from the windows.

As the Sinclairs gathered at the end of the day in their high room in Caithness Row they couldn't help laughing at each other. Everyone looked so odd. The three youngest children, who'd been in the school or the nursery, were grimy enough, but those who'd been working in the mill had legs and feet completely covered in sticky black oil. Their hair was white with cotton fluff. Their throats were dry and hoarse. Christina stood them each in turn in a basin of hot water and tried to scrub off the oil with a rough brush and a cake of yellow soap. Jockie kept grinning at Henny from a filthy face and boasting of his skill in creeping under the machines. He horrified them all with tales he'd heard from Donny of boys who'd lost their fingers or even their hands on those machines, and of others who'd been accidentally struck a terrible blow across the head by a broken belt from one of the pulleys. Henny told about her new friend, Effie MacQueen from the Isle of Skye, and about the powerful little monitor hanging over everyone's head. Betty talked of how her class had been taken for a walk up the green hillside to see the wild flowers and to learn their names and to listen to the birds' song. Tam had brought a small fife home with him and he drove the rest of the family mad by playing two shrill notes, over and over again. Wee Davie rocked backwards and forwards on his creepy, singing happy little songs to himself, while the rest of them talked and talked around him.

"It's the noise in yon mills I hate," protested Henny. "And all those machines grindin on and on and all those thousands of spindles goin round and round and all the white flue floatin in the air and the cardin engine shudderin like a horrible monster. The floors seem to shake underneath me in yon mill. And the big clock keeps such a hold on us all. I'd far sooner be at hame by the sea."

"We dinna have to go to the school, Mammie, do we?" asked Jockie. "I'm stane-tired."

"Nae, Jockie. Uncle James says next week'll be time enough to start at the school. Ye'll need a few days to settle into the work first. Yer friend Rab Cunningham spoke to me just as I was leavin the mill. He's comin here any minute to tak ye and Henny for a wee walk while it's still daylight. But eat up yer suppers first."

"I want to gang with Rab too!" shouted Betty. "He's my friend!"

Her mother shook her head.

"Nae, Betty," said her mother. "Henny and Jockie are older, remember."

Betty groaned.

"Older!" she muttered. "They're aye older! I'll never catch up wi them."

Now Rab was knocking on the door. He rushed in at once, his round face shining, his pale hair standing up on end.

"Come awa, the two of ye," he cried out to Henny and Jockie, pulling eagerly on their hands. "There's somethin I'm wantin to show ye!"

59

CHAPTER 5

Over the Wall

New Lanark, July 1819

"Where are we goin, Rab?" Henny asked him as the three of them ran down the stairway and out into the broad daylight of a long summer's evening. There had been heavy rain in mid-afternoon but now the sky was clear again.

"Wheesht!" whispered Rab, grinning at them happily. "It's a secret. Naebody kens the wood where I love to wander, except my grannie, but I'll show ye where it is. It'll be even more excitin if ye'll come there too. But ye must never tell a soul about it! Promise?"

Henny and Jockie nodded in agreement, still puzzled

about the mysterious place that Rab was leading them to.

"What's that man doin down there?" asked Jockie, stopping abruptly to peer through a basement window at a white-haired old man who sat working in the centre of a strange wooden cage that seemed to fill the whole room. He almost looked as if he were driving a cart.

"He's one o' the weavers," said Rab, "and yon's his loom. There's weavin families livin in maist o' the cellar rooms at New Lanark and dozens mair up in the wee houses in the Old Toun. The weavers work by hand, ye ken. Just watch him! When he pulls on that pickin handle in his right hand, ye can see the shuttle flyin backwards and forwards from side to side, weavin the weft in and out o' the warp. There's a pirn o' the best cotton thread from our own mills inside his shuttle. I heard the maister sayin that he might soon be bringin in some new kind o' looms. He says the power from our big water-wheels could easy throw the shuttles and drive the looms. My faither says it could bring awful trouble. It might put all our handloom weavers out o' work. Some folk might even break up the new-fangled looms wi axes and crowbars, my faither says."

Henny and Jockie didn't want to move. They stood gazing down through the open window in fascination as the weaver's shuttle leapt swiftly from left to right, from right to left, and as the weaver pulled the movable part of the frame towards him to change the position of the threads and then pushed it firmly back again. Henny noticed how the wood of his loom was shiny and smooth at the place where his hand had gripped it hundreds of times a day in a long lifetime of work.

"Come awa!" cried Rab impatiently, running on ahead. "I told ye. There's somethin far better than yon loom that I'm wantin ye to see!"

"Is it near the river?" whispered Henny excitedly, catching up with him and Jockie.

"Wheesht!" hissed Rab again, his finger on his lips, as they hurried over the mill-lade and then swung sharp left and up higher onto a narrow pathway under willow trees and alders. There, right beside them, was the river! Henny stopped and stared. White and muddy brown, the water surged over the stones, scouring the banks by the twisted alder roots and leaping helter-skelter downstream, past the backs of the cotton-mills and away to the distant sea. Jockie gasped in astonishment. This thundering river was far more powerful than their own quiet stream at home, with its gentle pools where salmon lurked in the shadows. This river was frightening.

"Just think what it'd be like if our mill-lade hadna taken half the water out already," said Rab, as Jockie and Henny both instinctively stepped back a few paces from the foaming torrent. "It's pretty full just now from all the summer rain we've been havin, but ye can guess what a winter's storm can do. Then we even hear the terrible roar of the river right up the hill in Old Lanark. My grannie says the maister's fine mills might be swept awa some mirk night!" Rab laughed out loud at the thought of it.

He ran quickly ahead of the others, giving them no time to stand any longer, excited and frightened, with their eyes fixed on the churning water.

"Would there be salmon here?" panted Jockie, trying to keep up with Rab.

"Na. They canna leap up the Stanebyres Falls, a bittie dounstream. But there's plenty fine eels and brown trout. Otters live by our river too, and kingfishers and cormorants. The Clyde's aye full o' life."

The water hurtled past them, a dangerous yellow underneath and foaming with froth on top. The edge of the river was alive with tiny white-chested dippers, fluttering, flying, bobbing about on the wet rocks and all along the muddy bank.

"Quiet!" hissed Rab softly, as the path started to climb. "We're comin to the wall."

"An old wall canna hear us!" laughed Henny, puffing up the steep slope.

"Na, it's the keeper that might hear us from over yon wall. But he's no often out so early in the evenin."

"The gamekeeper?" asked Jockie, full of new interest. "We've seen the keepers out on the moors near Wick. Have ye ever heard a keeper's pocket-watch, Rab? It strikes every half hour, even in the dark."

Rab nodded.

"Aye, I've heard it, but only the once," he said grimly. "I started runnin as fast as I could but the keeper caught me wi that terrible stick o' his."

Henny and Jockie opened their eyes wide in fear.

Now they came to the wall and stood looking up at it where it stood so high and solid, built of the same pink sandstone as the mills themselves.

"Is there a gate?" whispered Henny.

"Aye, there is. It's higher up this hillside where a road runs into the Bonnington estate but we canna gang that way. That's for the grand visitors, no for us. We'd have to pass the lodge that guards the gate and somebody'd be sure to see us. But I ken a bonny place where we can fly round the end o' the wall. Naebody'll see us at all. It's only a wee bit scary."

Rab turned sharp right and ran down beside the wall to a point overhanging the river. The wall came to a sudden end.

"We'll never get round there!" cried Henny, peering down at the swirling water below.

"We will," said Rab. "Look, I've made a fine wee hole for my hand on this side o' the wall and there's anither wee hole on tither side."

Jockie and Henny stared apprehensively at the small, neat hollow gouged out of the wall at head-height, very near its end.

"How do you fly around?" Henny asked, puzzled.

"Like this!" said Rab. "Ye put the fingers o' yer left hand into this hole and hold tight. Ye reach round the wall and put your right hand into tither hole. Then ye just swing yersel round and ye'll be in my secret wood."

"Ye swing over the edge o' yon roarin water?" exclaimed Jockie in disbelief.

Rab nodded confidently.

"Watch me," he said. "It's easy!"

Rab put his two hands into position and swung himself swiftly round the end of the wall as the river howled beneath him. Jockie and Henny could see him no longer.

"Come on!" he called softly from the far side. Henny and Jockie looked at each other in terror.

"What would our mammie say?" asked Henny.

"She'll no ken," said Jockie, pretending to be brave. "Will I gang first?"

"Aye," said Henny in relief.

Jockie put his fingers into the holes on each side of the wall. He leant back, kept his feet firm and swung himself out and around. Henny gasped. Then Jockie was gone.

"It's easy, Henny!" he whispered back to her. She thought his voice sounded very shaky all the same.

Now it was her turn. She gripped the wall in the two hollowed places. She swung herself out and around. The thundering brown water seemed so near. It roared in her ears. She shut her eyes. In an instant she was there! She was safe! Jockie grabbed her. Rab was grinning.

"How will we get back again?" she murmured.

"Same way!" said Rab. Henny and Jockie glanced at each other. Their eyes slid instantly to the river tumbling below.

"Come on!" said Rab.

"Will the keeper catch us here?" asked Jockie, peering through the thick trees ahead of them.

Rab kept his voice very soft.

"Na. I told ye. He disna come skulkin about in my secret woods while it's still daylight. He waits till later when it's dark and mirk. That's the time when poachers might be about. There's nae poachers from New Lanark. The maister's verra stern about poachin and trespassin. But there's a few wily men up in the Old Toun that sometimes slip down here after midnight to catch a rabbit or a pheasant. They sclim the wall with ropes. Yon Bonnington keeper kens weel when to catch them."

"Are ye a poacher yersel, Rab?" whispered Henny in admiration.

He shook his head.

"Na. I only come over the wall because there's somethin in these woods I like fine to look at," he murmured. "There's a stiff slope ahead of us but just walk along quick and quiet. We'll soon be there."

They climbed a path above the river under a thick green canopy of blackthorn and oak, elm and beech, holly and hazel. Henny and Jockie smelt the strong, rich scent of honeysuckle hanging all around them. Chaffinches and warblers flew away from their footsteps, startled into sudden movement. Bushy red squirrels scrambled up the tree trunks and looked down at them in surprise from between the leaves. Unexpectedly, Henny was seized again with that sharp painful memory of her father. He would have loved to wander through these woods with Rab. She wanted to cry.

Now Rab was leading them higher still, right above the dam, where the water lay smooth and black. He didn't pause an instant but hurried further on with a new, excited urgency.

"There!" he breathed softly as they stood at last on a ledge high over the water, just at a point where the river curved away in a sharp bend.

First Henny saw only a thick cloud of mist, a white haze of spray hanging high in the air. Her ears were battered by a deafening roar. Then she saw the waterfalls. Two great torrents of water, one behind the other, pouring down the rocky gorge ahead of them. Gigantic forest trees stretched up to the sky on either side, their branches festooned with green lichens, mosses and ferns.

"Corra Linn!" announced Rab. "And ye can just see a ruined old castle, high up on the far bank. Look!"

Through the mist, they caught a glimpse of the ruins but their eyes came swinging back again to the waterfalls. Corra Linn.

"Great folk travel from all over the world to look at these falls," said Rab proudly. "They want to see the mills too and they want to listen to the maister talkin on and on about all his new ideas, but maistly they want to see the falls. Poets come and painters and scientists and engineers and rich ladies and gentlemen. There's anither waterfall higher up at Bonnington Linn but I like Corra Linn best. I come here about twice a month at this time o' night, if I can slip awa from the school. I find a good place to sit by the edge of the river and I just stare and stare till my eyes are swimmin."

"Let's sit now," suggested Henny, looking around for a convenient stone. She wanted to look longer at the falls.

"Na, there's somethin else ye must see, Henny. We'll sclim up this wee path. All the maister's fine visitors come here in their satins and silks."

Jockie and Henny pulled themselves up to a square stone building perched high above the river. There were two wide windows, one above the other, on the side that faced the waterfall. There was a smaller window on each of the two side walls. The whole place looked to Henny like some kind of strange temple or a tiny church.

"The door's round at the back," whispered Rab. "The key's aye in the lock."

"I'm not sure I want to gang inside," said Henny nervously when she and Jockie had followed Rab round to the back and looked along an avenue of splendid lime trees that led right up to this mysterious building. Then she turned to face the solid door of this odd little house.

"It's perfitly safe!" Rab assured her with a quick smile. "The maister's visitors have gone back to their inn in Lanark and the grand folk at Bonnington House are eatin their supper just now. Then they play their music and sing their songs. I've heard them when I've been hidin under their windows. They never come near the waterfalls at this time o' the evenin."

Rab turned the key in the lock. He pushed the door open and led Henny and Jockie into a square room with its three windows and a fireplace in one corner.

"Keekin-glasses!" Rab cried with a triumphant laugh and a wave of his arm.

Jockie and Henny looked up. In every corner of the room and right across the high ceiling hung huge shining mirrors.

"What are they for?" asked Henny, puzzled.

"Sit down here with yer back to the window," said Rab, rushing to take a seat on the bench there himself. "Now, look up at the glasses!"

Jockie and Henny looked up. Henny shuddered and Jockie let out a sudden wild cry of fear. The mirrors reflected back into their eyes the full force of the Corra Linn falls. The roar of the real water came from behind them, out beyond the window, but inside the little stone room the rushing water seemed to be falling down on top of them, overwhelming them, drowning them.

When Henny's surge of giddiness had past, she turned to Rab in amazement.

"It's terrible!" she whispered in awe. "Why do all those rich folk want to come here to stare at this? Can they no just stand on the river bank and look straight at the falls the way we did? Why do they have to scare theirsels with mirrors?"

Rab chuckled to himself, quite unmoved by the torrent that seemed to come plunging down onto their heads inside this house of stone.

"I dinna ken why they do it," he said seriously. "I've asked my grannie. She says it might be because yon grand ladies and gentlemen are too scared to look straight at the falls, face to face like. They'd go all giddy and they'd swander with the shock. They might even tumble down into the river and be drouned! They're brought up verra soft, ye ken. So they just like to watch the falls in the keekin-glasses. That way they'll no be scared, my grannie says. They think it'll be like a hairmless picture in a frame. But my faither says my grannie's all wrong. He reckons the grand folk come here into the wee house because they're *wantin* to feel scared. He says it's far mair frightenin than lookin straight at the falls, and he says they enjoy it. I see what he means. I enjoy it mysel. It makes me go all shaky and shivery and oorie but I ken it canna hurt me at all. So then I laugh."

Henny closed her eyes. Jockie had his head in his hands.

"I dinna like it, Rab," he muttered, his voice breaking.

"Ye're a sapsie pair!" laughed Rab, dancing around the room, his eyes fixed on the terrifying reflections in the mirrors above him. "The great folk sit here for hours, ye ken. Their servants make tea and chocolate and coffee for them on a wee spirit stove in yon cellar below and carry it up here for the grand folk to drink. They sip it out of the best white cups."

"Let's go!" said Henny, leaping to her feet. "Maybe we'll come back some ither time, Rab. I canna quite get used to this place. Have ye been comin here for years?"

He nodded.

"I found it all for mysel," he said proudly. "The folk from the mills never come here. They want to please the maister and he's told them no to lowp over yon wall."

"Does he ken ye come here, Rab?" asked Jockie.

"Na, I take good care he disna ken a thing about it! Look, here's a book where the grand visitors sign their names."

Henny turned the pages of the big black book on a table. Dozens of strange names were scrawled or smudged or neatly inscribed. She only wished she could read them. Her father had always said he wanted her to be able to read one day, even though she was a girl, but she'd never gone to the school in Wick with Jockie. Perhaps she'd soon be learning to read in the mill-school at night. Her father would have been pleased about that.

"Come awa," cried Rab, pulling her eagerly away from

the book, "we'll run back to the wall along a higher path. We might find some wild strawberries up there. They're the sweetest thing in all the world! Later there'll be brambles and blaeberries and puddock-stools, and then there'll be the hazel nuts. There's aye somethin good to eat in the woods. There's plants to cure all sorts o' sickness as well. My grannie tells me which leaves to bring hame to her whenever I come here."

Rab locked the door behind him and left the key in its lock. Then off he ran, making for a higher path to lead them back to the wall.

They hurried along in silence, not speaking at all, their minds still full of the hurtling waterfall and the mirrors that magnified it. Suddenly Henny shot out one arm and grabbed Rab.

"Look!" she whispered. "What is it?"

Rab stood utterly still. Jockie froze beside him. Only a few paces away, a solid little animal with a black-and-white-striped face was edging backwards down a narrow pathway of her own, dragging a thick bundle of dry grass that she gripped tightly with her front paws and her chin. The fur on her back was almost grey but her feet were black.

"Brock!" breathed Rab. "There's a sett nearby. Dinna move. That's the sow."

They fixed their eyes on the energetic badger as she hauled her untidy clump of grass down the slope towards a dark oval hole in the hillside. With a sudden swift turn of her body, she disappeared into the hole, pulling the bundle in with her.

"That's grass for her beddin," said Rab when the badger had gone. "We'll come back again to watch her some ither night. We might see the whole family next time. This is a grand time to find the brocks. In the gloamin as the light's fadin."

"She moves a bit like a weasel," Jockie said. "So quick on her feet and snuffin the air with that long nose of hers and turnin her head so fast."

Soon they were back at the wall. Henny's heart sank but Rab ran down its whole length to the end over the river, thrust his fingers into the two holes and swung himself to the other side. Jockie followed him without a second's pause, and then, with a gasp of fear, came Henny.

"I'm never never goin into yon woods again, Rab!" she said, her arms still trembling from her fierce grip on the wall. Her knees were shaking. Rab laughed.

"I think ye will, Henny," he said. "The longer ye work in yon mill, the sooner ye'll be longin to go back to my secret woods. But dinna tell yer minnie about the place. I'll tak ye again some fine night but naebody must ken a thing about it or we'd soon be stopped. I love to wander in yon woods and my grannie disna mind. Most nights I'm in the school, but now and then I just troon the school and sclim round the wall. My woods are naethin like the mills."

Henny couldn't help smiling in agreement. She thought of those thousands of stiff spindles, twirling round and round so fast the whole day long. She thought of the rows of clanking machines. She thought of the turning rollers and the wide running belts, the endless hiss and hum of the great water-wheels under the mills, the smell of oil and cotton in her nostrils and the dry taste of fluff at the back of her throat. She thought of Kelly's clock with its five round faces, keeping strict time for the whole village. Then she remembered Corra Linn and its free, rushing water, the mist in the air and the wet ferns hanging from the tree-trunks. That wild river knew nothing about clocks or spindles! She remembered the careful badger with her bundle of grass. She remembered the fresh smell of leaves and the sweet scent of honeysuckle. Rab had shown her an utterly different world over the high stone wall. In spite of the fearful swing over dangerous water, Henny knew that she wanted to go back into that other world. And soon!

CHAPTER 6

⚭ ⚭ ⚭ ⚭ ⚭

Jockie

New Lanark, August 1819

A week later, Jockie could hardly remember Rab's secret woods over the wall. He had almost forgotten the wild waterfall and the badgers' sett and the tiny house of mirrors. All he could think about now was the oily floor of the mill where he spent six long days every week, slithering about under the spinning mules with his brush and his pan, endlessly sweeping and sweeping. At first he'd thought the job was great fun – he'd laughed and joked with the other boys – but the fun soon wore off. Cotton fluff in his throat made him cough almost as badly as Uncle James. Black oil was ingrained in his knees, his feet, his hands, his face, his hair, in spite of his mother's rough scrubbings every night. He began to long for a change from sweeping the floors to oiling the spindles. He envied those boys who ran around the mill with their long-spouted oil-cans, dragging the nozzle hard along every row of spindles and making a tremendous racket. Jockie wanted to make a noise like that. He even asked Willie Grant politely if he could have a try at oiling the spindles but the overseer shook his head.

"Na! It's far too soon, laddie. Stick to the sweepin. Ye're no near quick enough yet."

So Jockie crawled about even more speedily under the machines and wielded his brush still faster. He gave up chatting to the other boys. He kept his mind on his work. Day by day, the overseer turned Jockie's silent monitor that hung near the spinning mule where his mother was working. First he moved it from black to blue and then from blue to yellow.

"Ye're a good lad," Willie Grant said approvingly. "Keep at it!"

On the happy morning when Jockie found his monitor set to white, he grinned with pride.

"Look at this, Mammie!" he shouted out to her in triumph, pointing up to his wee block of wood. "Mine's white! And yers is only yella!"

"Stop yer bletherin, Jockie Sinclair!" the overseer bellowed right in his ear. "I'm turnin yer monitor back to yella this verra minute! And I'm turnin yer mither's to white. She's a good mill-hand."

Jockie was quite crestfallen. He groaned out loud and

rubbed hot tears of envy from his eyes with an oily hand. Now his mother was the one who was smiling. She was glad that Willlie Grant had stopped Jockie from so much foolish boasting. That was exactly what his father would have wanted for the boy.

Christina Sinclair herself was working quite easily with her spinning machine now. Her 'Jeanie'. All her new friends in the mill fondly called their own machines their 'Jeanies', so Christina did the same. She sang softly to herself as she moved confidently up and down her rows of whirling spindles, always keeping one sharp eye on Jockie to make sure he was hard at work and not wasting time. Her ears had even grown accustomed to the terrible racket of the mill. She hardly noticed it now. But sometimes in the middle of the night she thought she could still hear the noise of all those machines, clanking somewhere deep inside her head.

On the day when Jockie's monitor had suddenly been turned back from white to yellow, Mr Robert Owen himself came walking briskly through the mill. Two well-dressed ladies followed close behind him, lifting the hems of their long skirts just off the oily floor. The master stopped abruptly by Jockie's monitor and then looked down with kind but sorrowful eyes at the boy who was huddled right underneath his machine.

"Only yellow?" Mr Owen said sadly. "Have you not been working well, boy? What's the trouble?"

Jockie felt ashamed of himself. His face flushed red under the black oil.

"I'm verra sorry, sir," he said quickly, sliding out on his

knees and then standing up to face the master honestly. "My wee monitor was white, sir, but then I was boastin and bletherin far too much and the overseer turned it back to yella. I'll no be wasting mair time wi bletherin, sir."

"Good lad! That's the right spirit! Have you thought any more about coming up to Braxfield House to be our odd-job boy? There's another lad who wants the position so I can't let you take too long to make up your mind."

Jockie made a quick decision.

"Aye, sir," he said. "I have been thinkin. I'd like fine to come to yer house. I'd work verra hard for ye, sir."

The master nodded in approval and turned to the two ladies who were examining Jockie's smeared face with interest.

"You see how well my system works, dear ladies! This boy is not stupid, but it's taken him a while to settle down properly and to stop wasting time in idle chatter. My overseer didn't need to use any harsh beatings to bring him to his senses. This clever little block of wood has done the trick. The boy wants to work well now, don't you, lad?"

"Aye, sir, I want to work better and better every day." Jockie's white teeth flashed into a sudden smile as he looked up at the master. He knew what Mr Owen would like to hear.

"Right, boy. Finish this week here in the mill first. If your monitor is turned to white again by Saturday at the latest, you can start at my house next Monday morning. Be sure you're knocking on our back door at six o'clock sharp. All right?"

"Aye, sir. I'll be there at day-daw!" And Jockie laughed out loud with happiness.

The master bent down to pick up a fleck of white cotton lying on the floor. Solemnly he handed it to Jockie who put it into his pan. As Mr Owen walked on through the mill with his two elegant guests, the ladies were exclaiming in whispered astonishment to each other.

"What a wonderfully kind way Mr Owen has with these poor, ignorant children," said the first. "They actually want to work well to please him."

"Yes," said the other. "If only the cruel masters in those shocking Manchester mills would try Mr Owen's new methods, the world would be a better place!"

And, as they swept on their way, both ladies turned their heads to take one last look at Jockie who was already hard at work again, crawling eagerly under the spinning machines with his little brush and pan.

Mr Owen led his visitors upstairs to watch the scutchers at work, cleaning the raw cotton in a cloud of white dust. Henny's monitor had just been turned to white. The master smiled his approval the minute he saw it.

"Well done, girl!" he cried in delight. "You're another one of those new Sinclairs from Wick, aren't you? I can see you're going to make a fine mill-hand. I hope you'll stay on here in New Lanark for sixty years or more! Would you like to spend your whole life in my splendid mills, girl?"

Henny nodded politely but she was silently hoping she'd be safely back in Wick long before sixty years had passed. She'd found the only way to get through each dreary day was to keep her mind on Rab's mysterious woods over the wall. Scared as she was at the thought of whirling around the end of that wall again, she was desperately hoping that Rab would soon take her back there so she could watch the badgers foraging in the fading light and gaze at the thundering waterfall in its cloud of mist. She wanted to listen to the river-birds calling and to smell the scent of wildflowers under those ancient trees. The two ladies smiled kindly at Henny, the model worker, who was going to spend sixty happy years in Mr Owen's wonderful mills. They had no idea what she was really thinking.

By Saturday morning, Jockie's monitor had been turned to white at last. His new job for the master was certain. On Sunday afternoon, when the long church service was over, Rab offered to take the whole Sinclair family for a walk but not upstream to his high wall. This time he led them downstream quite a way and then up a sloping gravel path from the river's edge. They came to a place where they could stand together, well hidden under newly planted trees, a respectful distance from Braxfield House.

"Yon's the place where ye'll be workin the morn, Jockie!" Rab exclaimed. Christina Sinclair and her children gazed in silent awe. It certainly was a magnificent house.

At the centre of the mansion, under a steep tiled roof, was the main wing. There were four long windows on the upper floor and four below. The front door was exactly in the middle. From each end of this building, another wing ran back at right angles.

"How many families are livin there, Rab?" Henny asked him as her eyes swept along the majestic roofs and the elegant windows.

"Just Mr Robert Owen's family and all their servants," Rab answered. "A family like the Owens needs plenty o' space, ye ken. They couldna live in one room. My faither went right inside yon house once to mend the maister's big clock on the turn of the stairs. He saw everythin! There's a drawin room on one side, he told me, and a dinin room on tither. They keep hundreds o' bottles o' red wine in the cellar underneath. There's a grand bedroom over the drawin room and a library over the dinin room. The library's the place where the maister keeps all his books, ye ken. Thousands o' books, my faither said, all bound in leather. Mr Owen's lads and lassies each have their own bedrooms in one o' yon side-wings and the servants sleep in the attics."

"I canna go knockin at the fine front door, Rab!" Jockie said with a puzzled frown. "The maister told me to come to the back door."

"I'll show ye," Rab said, confident as ever. "We'll walk a bittie behind the house and then ye'll see into the back courtyard. That's where ye'll find the stables and the barn and the dairy and the coal-shed and the kitchen door and everythin else."

Henny's eyes opened wide at this long list of Rab's.

"The maister's house is as big as a whole town!" she said in astonishment. "And how strange to be one o' the maister's ain lassies wi a room all to hersel for sleepin in! It must be awful lanely!"

Keeping well under the trees, the family skirted right around Braxfield House until they were looking down at its high back fence. The gate stood wide open.

"Yon's the way ye'll walk in, Jockie," Rab said, pointing to the gate. "And then ye'll gang through the courtyard. Ye'll knock on the kitchen door. See, it's green."

Jockie nodded solemnly, his eyes fixed on the kitchen door. He felt wildly excited about the new job he'd be starting the next day but he was scared too. What exactly might be waiting for him behind that green door?

"It's sure to be better than sweepin in the mill, Jockie," Henny whispered to him, reading his thoughts.

Early the next morning, even before the first bell had begun to ring, Jockie was up and dressed in his clean mill-clothes. He hugged his mother and Henny and the younger ones and then set off on his new run past the mills, along the river-bank, up between the trees to the master's house and around to the courtyard at the back. He knocked on the green kitchen door at six o'clock exactly, just as the second bell down at the mills had stopped its ringing. A tall, stout man with grey hair opened the door.

"Ah," he said, looking carefully at Jockie. "The new boy. Right on time! Come in, lad. You can eat a dish of porridge with the rest of us before you start your work. You don't have to wear those mill-clothes here at the house, you know. Miss Drysdale will find you something more suitable."

Jockie followed the stout man into the kitchen, where twelve servants were seated around a long table, all eating their breakfast.

"This is the new odd-job lad," the stout man announced. "The master chose him at the mill. His name's Jockie Sinclair." Twelve pairs of eyes turned to stare at Jockie.

"Ye can sit by me, Jockie," a friendly girl said to him with a smile. He slid into the empty chair beside her.

"There's Miss Drysdale at the top of the table," the man explained to the new boy. "She's the master's housekeeper. I'm the butler. Sheddon's the name. We'll be teaching you your new job. If you're quick to learn, you can stay on here for years. If you're slow in the uptake, you'll be back in the mill in a couple of weeks. Do you understand?"

Jockie shivered as he nodded. He hoped he'd be quick in the uptake. He glanced at the thin woman at the far end of the table, Miss Drysdale. She looked quite stern. Her steely grey hair was wound back into a tight bun on the nape of her neck. Her long black dress was buttoned to her throat. She did not smile but gave Jockie a curt nod of welcome. Then she put out one hand to pat the plump fingers of a red-eyed, older boy who was sitting close beside her. He was a heavy, ungainly boy. He glowered at Jockie and went on spooning porridge into his wide mouth.

That first day was not easy. As Jockie tried to remember which room was which and who was who among the servants, he also had to find out how to fill the hods with coal in the coal house and where to carry them. He had to discover where to tip the cold ashes from every fireplace in the house and how to set the new fires. The house was quite cold, even in mid-summer, and fires were lit each evening. He had to fill large jugs of clean water for every bedroom and toss away the dirty water. He had to empty the chamber pots, clean the shoes and polish the silver. He had to visit the dairy, the stables, the barn, the cellar and the butler's pantry, while Mr Sheddon himself explained to him carefully where tools and brushes were kept.

"A place for everything, Jockie Sinclair, and everything in its place!" said the butler sternly. "That's what the master likes, and that's how we run this house!" Jockie tried to remember all he had been told in one crowded morning.

At the very end of the day, after the last meal had been eaten, when the housekeeper had withdrawn to her own private room and the butler had joined his wife and family in their quarters upstairs, the servants sat about chatting happily to each other in the warm kitchen. Jockie kept quiet, listening to what everyone said. At nine o'clock, the butler came down again and put his head in at the door.

"Bed!" he said.

Immediately, every servant picked up a candlestick and lit the candle. Then they all trooped up the back stairs to their attics. Jockie followed the men and boys to a long room over the north wing.

"New boy!" the groom called out to him, forgetting his name. "Ye'll be sharin this bed with Dan."

Jockie pulled off his clothes, folded them neatly, blew out his candle and jumped into one end of the narrow bed just as the older boy, who'd been sitting next to the housekeeper at every meal in the kitchen that day, climbed into the other end. With the rough blankets right up to his neck, Jockie soon felt warm and comfortable. He lay as still as a stone and wondered what Henny and the others were doing down in the family's whitewashed room by the mills. He felt a bit lost and homesick. He was just beginning to drift off to sleep when the big boy at the far end of his bed kicked him sharply in the shins. Jockie took no notice though he certainly felt the pain. It must have been an accident, he thought to himself. Five minutes later came another kick, much harder this time. Jockie still made no movement and gave no cry. But when a third kick came, even more violent than the second, he yelped out loud in agony. He was sure now that the big boy must have kicked him on purpose. White with fury, he sat up in bed.

Moonlight was streaming in through the windows. Jockie glared at the boy who lay peacefully at the other end of the bed with his eyes closed and an unpleasant grin on his lips.

"Hey!" hissed Jockie. "You! Boy! Dan! Stop kickin me!"

A muffled snigger came from the big boy's pillow.

"Right!" said Jockie. "I can kick too, ye ken."

He slid back under the blanket and let fly with both legs at once. Dan leapt from the bed with a howl of pain. The other six servants in the attic, men and boys, sat up at once to see what the trouble was.

"He kicked me!" Dan moaned, hopping round the attic, clutching his knee. His broad face was trembling. His pale eyes were open wide.

"He kicked me first!" shouted Jockie. "Three times he kicked me!"

One of the men came to sort out the trouble.

"Surely ye ken why poor Dan Drysdale's kickin ye, laddie."

"Na, I dinna ken!" said Jockie indignantly. "I've done him nae harm. I've never said a word to him all day!"

"But he wanted yer job, see," the man explained patiently. "Dan's been workin out in the maister's garden for these past two years but he's been wantin badly to work inside the house, see, bringin in the coal, cleanin the shoes, settin the tables, polishin the silver. Miss Drysdale's his auntie, see. She told Dan he'd be sure to get the inside job when the last boy had to go, but then suddenly the maister gied it to ye, see. That's why Dan Drysdale's kickin ye."

"It's no fair!" cried Jockie. "I'll tell the maister tomorrow!"

"Na, na! Dinna do that!" said the man in alarm. "The maister canna abide us bickerin and fechtin. He'll be lecturin us for hours if ye tell him, see. He wants the whole world to stop its fechtin! Peace and harmony, see! That's what he wants! We'll just work it out for oursels, see. Ye can go and sleep at the end of wee Georgie's bed. Georgie never kicks. We'll leave Dan to lie here all on his lane. Ye must steer clear o' Dan in the daytime or he'll ding ye. He's aye dingin one o' the lads. We canna stop him, see. He goes straight to tell his auntie if we try. Then we're in awful trouble, see."

Jockie moved across to the other side of the attic and

climbed into the end of wee Georgie's bed. He settled down again to sleep and tried to keep back the hot tears that ran from his eyes. The attic was quiet now apart from an occasional snuffle of triumphant laughter from Dan Drysdale. Jockie could hear the women servants and the girls talking quietly together in the attic next door.

"Tak no notice o' yon Dan!" wee Georgie whispered urgently, "or he'll ding us all."

Jockie slept at last.

Over the next two weeks, Jockie's life began to fall into a regular rhythm at Braxfield House. He was quick to learn and he soon knew what he had to do at each hour of every day. He kept well clear of Dan Drysdale and there was no more trouble. On Sunday afternoons he was free at last to run down the hill after church to spend a few hours with his family, so long as he was back at Braxfield by seven o'clock. Mr Sheddon, the butler, was certainly pleased with him.

"I've told the master you're doing well, lad," he said in the kitchen one day, patting him gently on the head and smiling benignly down at him. "Mr Owen's made a good choice."

Jockie could hardly wait till the next Sunday to tell his mother the good news. Christina Sinclair beamed with pride to hear that her son was making such a fine impression up at the big house.

"Yer dear faither would've been glad, Jockie," she said. "He'd want ye to be honest and quick and hard-workin."

A week later, on a warm afternoon, Mr Sheddon sent Jockie to walk under a thick clump of trees behind Braxfield House to gather wood for the fires. He was staggering back to the house with his arms full when Dan Drysdale suddenly confronted him.

"Put down yer logs, laddie!" Dan roared at him. "I'm goin to fecht ye!"

"Na!" said Jockie, feeling frightened but determined to be brave, "The maister disna like us to fecht, Dan."

"I dinna care what the maister likes or disna like! Ye've taken my job and I'm goin to fecht ye. Put down yer logs and put up yer fists!"

Jockie dropped his bundle of wood and stood face to face with the bigger boy. Before he'd had time to think, Dan had punched him on the nose. Blood spurted out in a long red stream. Jockie punched back but missed his aim. Then Dan's fist hit him straight in the eye. Jockie wanted to turn and run but he tried one more blow. This time it hit home. Dan reeled back for a second but then came charging forward, his head down low, ready to ram Jockie in the stomach.

"Stop!" cried a voice. A firm hand pulled Jockie backwards.

"It's the maister!" gasped Dan, standing to attention, stiff and upright, with a look of complete innocence on his broad face.

"Dan Drysdale and Jockie Sinclair!" cried Mr Owen in shocked tones. "Two boys from my own household, fighting like dogs in the woods! I can hardly believe it. Who started this fight? Tell me the truth now!"

"It was him, sir!" Dan blurted out at once. "First he kicked me in bed and now he's punched me in the face."

"Na, na, it wasna me, sir!" said Jockie indignantly.

"There's to be no fighting at all!" explained the master. "If anyone hits you, Dan Drysdale, what should you do?"

"Turn the ither cheek, sir," Dan said promptly. "It's in the Bible!"

"If only all the quarrelling nations of the world would listen to you, Dan, what a happy world it would be!" Mr Owen said earnestly.

Dan nodded. The master turned to Jockie.

"I'm disappointed in you, boy. I'd expected better things of you. I didn't think you were a lad to get yourself into foolish fights. I'll give you only one more chance. If ever I catch you fighting again, you'll go straight back to the mill. This boy, Dan, has had a hard life. Both his parents are dead. Miss Drysdale, my excellent housekeeper, is his only relative. What Dan needs is kindness, not punches. Do you understand me, Jockie?"

"Aye, sir," Jockie said, meekly enough. He was seething within.

"Follow Dan's good advice, boy, and always turn the other cheek. Do you hear me?"

"Aye, sir," said Jockie, rubbing his own aching cheek and using his sleeve to mop up the blood that still dripped from his nose.

"Shake hands now, boys!" said Mr Owen. "That's the only proper way to end a fight."

Dan was eager to hold out his hand. Jockie was reluctant but he did it at last.

"Good lads," said the master. "Back to your work now and be good friends."

Mr Owen strode off. Dan sniggered.

"I'll never be your friend, Jockie Sinclair!" he hissed. He turned away and lumbered back to the house. Jockie followed more slowly.

CHAPTER 7

Dan Drysdale

New Lanark, August 1819

That same evening, Jockie appeared at supper in Braxfield House with one black eye and a swollen nose. He glanced apprehensively at the other servants around the table. Dan Drysdale was not there.

"Have you been fighting, Jockie Sinclair?" Mr Sheddon demanded sternly as Jockie sat down in his usual place.

"Aye sir, but the maister caught us and he's told us we're no to fecht ony mair. He made us promise, sir."

"Us?" asked the butler. "Who exactly were you

fighting with, lad?"

Jockie opened his mouth to answer when Miss Drysdale interrupted him.

"There's no need for the poor boy to tell us any tales, Mr Sheddon. As Mr Owen has dealt with him already, I don't think we should pry any further. Whoever the other boy was, I'm sure he and Jockie will be good friends from now on. Isn't that right, Jockie?"

Jockie nodded but without much enthusiasm.

"Good boy," said Miss Drysdale, giving him a bleak smile. "Eat up your bread now and you'll soon feel better."

Straight after breakfast the next morning, Miss Drysdale sent Jockie out to the coal-house to fill up the hods with coal. He didn't much like the coal-house. It was dark in there. The smell of coal was acrid. He propped the door open wide to let in as much daylight as he could and felt his way slowly forwards with his shovel till he came to the pile of coal right at the back of the shed. He dug deep into the coal and tipped the solid black lumps into his first hod.

Suddenly, without warning, a heavy weight came crashing down onto the back of his head. Jockie bellowed out loud in shock and pain as he fell to the floor. His face sank into the coal-dust. He lay still.

A boy with pale eyes climbed quietly down from the pile of coal, a shinty stick in his hand. He glided to the door. He was just slinking out into the sunlight, brushing the coal from his clothes, when an all too familiar voice stopped him.

"Dan Drysdale!" said Mr Owen kindly. "What was that terrible cry? Are you hurt at all, my boy? Come closer so I can see you properly."

Dan dropped his stick and came closer, his face flushed, his eyes on the ground.

"Bring me that stick," said the master.

Dan turned to pick up the stick and carried it reluctantly to Mr Owen. The master ran his fingers over the stick.

"There's blood on this stick, boy!" said the master in alarm.

Dan was silent. Suddenly Mr Owen went striding off to the coal-house.

"Wait there!" he called back sharply to Dan.

The master stumbled over Jockie's body in the coal-house. He bent down and peered at the boy's face in the half-light.

"It's Jockie Sinclair!" he murmured to himself in surprise. "Not again!"

Mr Owen slipped one arm under Jockie's shoulders and another under his knees. He carried him out of the coal-house and straight into the kitchen. He lifted him onto the long bare table.

"Miss Drysdale!" he called. "Send someone for the surgeon this minute. And bring a dish of water. Be quick, woman! This boy's been attacked in the coal-house."

Miss Drysdale moved swiftly. There was fear in her eyes. She sent wee Georgie running to the mills to find the surgeon and brought a white towel and a basin of cold water to the master.

"Is the poor laddie deid?" she gasped, guessing at once who had wielded the stick.

"He's breathing but only just. You clean up this wound now while I put a blanket over him. Such a bright boy too. So willing to learn. So quick and honest with his tongue but never rude. I was sure he'd go a long way, if he didn't get caught up in silly quarrels. I had great plans for him, Miss Drysdale. That's why I gave him this job in the house. And now, who knows if he'll live?"

The housekeeper's face was white. Her hands were shaking as she dipped one end of her towel into the water and carefully washed the blood away from the wound on Jockie's head. "Dan never means any trouble, sir," she murmured politely when she had finished. She held a tiny bottle of smelling salts under Jockie's nose. Jockie shivered and sneezed though his eyes were still shut.

"Oh yes, he did mean trouble this time, Miss Drysdale! I warned Dan yesterday and just now I found him with the stick in his hand. He'll have to go."

"Go!" gasped the housekeeper. "Oh, please give him one more chance, sir," she begged. "You could talk to him, perhaps. He's sure to take notice of you, sir. Or your good wife could talk to him. You see sir, Dan's been brought up so badly. My brother was always far too hard on him. He wouldn't listen to your wonderful new ideas about treating children kindly and gently. He was forever beating the poor lad."

"That's always the way," said the master sadly, his sympathy now swinging suddenly back towards Dan. "First the parents beat the children and then the children beat each other and then the nations go to war. Violence breeds violence! Somehow I'll have to change all that but it's a long struggle. Twenty years I've been at it, Miss Drysdale! Twenty years!"

The master sank into a chair beside Jockie and sat there, gloomily sighing to himself, his big soft eyes fixed as if mesmerized on the boy's swelling wound. Half an hour later the surgeon came running in through the door, bag in hand, a tall thin man with a smooth face. Carefully he examined Jockie's head, pushing back the dark hair to see the bruises and the broken skin. He clicked his tongue mournfully.

"It's bad, sir," he said. "Very bad. But there's a faint flicker in those eyelids. I think he's coming round. Make a pot of tea, Miss Drysdale. He'll be needing it soon. I'll put a dressing and a bandage on his head and raise him up a bit on a pile of pillows. Then we'll see. I think you'd better send for his mother, Mr Owen, or someone in his family. If he has any family."

"He has," said the master. "A fine new family, from Wick. Miss Drysdale, send that Georgie off again. To the mills this time. Number Two. This boy's mother's working at the spindles. Christina Sinclair's her name. There's a girl somewhere, too. Red hair. Ask the overseer. Find one or the other and bring her up here."

Mr Owen turned back to Jockie whose eyes were open now, staring around the big kitchen in confusion.

"The coal-house!" Jockie murmured. "I canna see the coal!"

He moved his head and cried out in terror at the

94

sudden pain.

"Lie still, laddie," said the surgeon. "Forget about the coal for now. You'll be fine. Your mother's coming from the mill."

Jockie closed his eyes again. His brain seemed to be spinning out of control. He groaned out loud.

Christina Sinclair ran the whole way up the long sloping hill from the mills to Braxfield House, her skirt hitched high in her hands, her lips pressed tightly together. "Some kind of accident", was all she'd been told by Georgie, and she was still trying to puzzle out what it could possibly be. She'd been so sure that Jockie would be safe from all accidents in a well-run household like the master's grand mansion. The children working in the mill were in far more danger, or so she had thought. A finger or a hand or even an arm might get caught in a moving belt or a rolling mule. And those high mills had so many steps and stairs to tumble down. But in Mr Owen's own home, where his wife was sure to preside calmly over her family of growing sons and daughters, where the housekeeper and the butler would make sure everything always ran smoothly! How could Jockie come to any harm in a place like that? It was a mystery.

Georgie ran beside her, excited to have been the bearer of bad tidings but having little idea what had really happened.

"Yer lad was as good as deid when the maister carried him in, Missus!" he said dramatically as he pushed open the back gate.

Christina gave a cry of fear and ran faster still. At the green door she paused and knocked. Mr Owen himself had just gone. It was Miss Drysdale who led her into the kitchen, anxious to say as little as possible about the accident.

"Here he is!" she cried in pretended cheerfulness, pointing to the boy still stretched out on the kitchen table, his eyes closed, a bandage around his head, a blanket over his shivering body.

"Jockie!" gasped his mother in horror. "Whatever's happened to ye?"

Jockie opened his eyes. A slow lopsided smile spread over his whole face.

"Mammie!" he murmured and took her hand. "I want to go hame. Hame to the sea!"

"We canna go back to the sea, dearie. The sea's gone forever. But I'm sure ye could come back to our new hame by the mill. If we can only find some kind folk to carry ye there. Perhaps the maister would let me stay off work for a few days, to look after ye till ye're feelin better."

"I'm sure he will," said Miss Drysdale quickly. "I'll ask him myself this evening. And I'll send for the gardeners now to make some sort of stretcher to carry the poor lad down to the village. The sooner he's back home, the better he'll be."

"But what was it exactly that happened to my Jockie?" asked Christina, looking the housekeeper in the eyes.

"I'm not too sure," said Miss Drysdale, her voice trembling a little. "Perhaps the master knows more about it. Do sit down now. Here's a chair. I'll call the gardeners."

Christina sank onto the hard wooden chair and took Jockie's small hands in hers.

"Ye'll soon be safe at hame, dearie," she said. "Ye needna come back to work here at the maister's house. Ye can work in the mill with Henny. Ye'll like that far better."

"Na, Mammie," Jockie protested faintly. "I'm wantin to work here. I canna let him win."

"Who?" said his mother, startled, but Jockie made no answer.

Two sturdy gardeners came into the kitchen carrying an old wooden door to use as a stretcher. Christina walked behind them all the way down to Caithness Row and up the stairs to their own room.

"He's a promisin lad, Missus," said the head gardener as she thanked them both. "We heard the maister say so. Mr Owen's got grand plans for that lad."

"But Jockie'd only been there for a few days!" she said in surprise. "How could the maister ken anythin about him?"

"Mr Owen's aye quick to tak tent o' a bright lad or lassie," said the man. "He can tell by the look in their eyes, we reckon. The maister made an early start in life hissel, ye ken. He left his hame in Wales to be apprentice to a draper when he was only ten year old and he's never looked back. He'll want your Jockie to have a good chance in life."

"If he ever gets better," she said sadly.

"The surgeon'll be here again tomorrow, Missus, and ye willna have to pay a single penny. Dinna fash about the lad. He's a tough wee manikin and he'll soon recover. He comes from Caithness, after all, and so do we. We've baith been pulled half-drouned from the sea many a time, and we're still alive to tell the tale."

Christina Sinclair smiled at the two men and thanked them. Their voices were comfortable and kind. As they left the room, she sat down beside her son where he lay on one of the hurlie-beds.

"Jockie," she said, putting her arms right around him. "Tell me what happened." Jockie told her. Dan Drysdale, the housekeeper's nephew. The kicking in the bed. The fighting in the woods. The master's stern words when he'd caught them at it. The sudden blow in the coalhouse. He couldn't remember the rest.

"Ye're never goin back to that shockin house!" Christina said indignantly. "Yon Dan's a murtherer!"

"But, Mammie," Jockie protested faintly. "The maister says Dan's had a sair life. We must be verra kind to him!"

"Blethers! Ye've had a sair life yersel, Jockie, with yer faither drowned at sea! Most Caithness folk have a sair life. Yon Dan disna deserve any pity at all!"

"Faither wouldna wish me to be a feardie, Mammie! He'd tell me to run back to the maister's house when my heid's mended!"

Christina was silent. She knew that what Jockie said was true. Her husband had been a brave man himself. He wouldn't want the lad to be a coward.

"We'll see, Jockie," she said at last. "We'll wait till yer poor heid's mended."

CHAPTER 8

Visitors

New Lanark, early September 1819

Three weeks later, just as Henny was catching the first whiff of autumn in the air, Jockie was back at Braxfield House. He had recovered well enough, apart from a jagged white scar across the back of his head.

"The hair'll soon grow and hide it, Jockie," the other servants at Braxfield assured him whenever they saw him frowning as he ran his finger gently along the scar.

Jockie's life at the master's house was quite different now. Miss Drysdale was stern towards him but never unkind. She could see that Mr Owen liked the boy so there was no point in her treating him badly. All was peaceful in the servants' attic at night. Dan Drysdale had gone! The master had packed him off to work in the mills. The overseer in Number Two had given Dan a long-handled broom and set him to sweeping the stairways and keeping the mill privies clean. Dan was furious. He'd thought he was set for life in Braxfield House. He'd even had his eye on Mr Sheddon's job as butler in the years ahead, but now all those hopes were dashed. He glowered and grumbled as he dragged his broom reluctantly down every step from the top floor of the mill to the basement, gathering dust and wisps of cotton into tidy piles and scraping them into his pan. He scowled as he had to go into the privy on every level to scrub the floor and the wooden seat till they were spotlessly clean. Worse still, towards the end of the day he had to help another scavenger to carry the full cans down to the street, ready for the night-cart. Early the next morning he had to bring up the empty cans. Dan hated the whole job. It was Jockie he blamed.

Instead of sleeping in the luxury of the servants' attic at Braxfield House, Dan now had to board with a family of strangers from the Highlands. They gave him three meals a day and the spare end of a bed for sleeping. The MacDonalds were kind people and made him welcome in their room up a stair in Double Row, but their meals were nothing like as good as the ones he had eaten in Mr Owen's house. They always chattered away to each other in Gaelic as they sat around their table and Dan had no idea what they were talking about. So he took to wandering off by himself every evening from suppertime till bedtime. He slouched along the river's edge below the mills, muttering angrily to himself as he kicked away loose stones or threw them at the birds.

Dan wished that the Sinclair family had never come to New Lanark. How could he get rid of them? Some secret way so no-one would suspect him at all. Then Mr Owen would be sure to take him back into Braxfield House again, he thought. Dan's pale eyes gleamed with new hope as he shuffled up and down the stairs of Mill Number Two with his broom.

But as the long days began to shorten, Jockie was almost happy. He knew nothing of Dan's sour thoughts. In fact, he had forgotten about Dan altogether. Every morning at Braxfield House, after he had cleaned the fireplaces and carried out the ashes and brought in fresh coals and set new fires for the day, Mr Sheddon would take him into the dining room where the long polished table was set with fine china plates, delicate glassware, splendid candelabra and silver knives and forks. The butler kept his face always stiff and serious as he made Jockie stand with him by each chair in turn, checking that everything on the table was in its proper place. At first Jockie was bewildered by this daily ritual but gradually he learnt exactly where each fork, each glass, each dish should be. Mr Sheddon watched with a careful eye as Jockie stretched out his hand to move a salt-cellar slightly to the left or a serving spoon slightly to the right.

"Well done, lad," he would murmur in quiet approval, rubbing his hands together and almost allowing a faint smile to crack his face. "We'll make a good butler of you one of these days, so long as you don't get itchy feet and run off to sea."

Jockie smiled to himself. He still often thought about the sea but he was starting to enjoy this new life at Braxfield House. Within a few weeks, he knew the names and faces of all the master's children and would bow politely if he happened to meet any one of them in the passageway. Mrs Owen herself had stopped him one day and asked if his head was completely better. He'd even heard from the other servants about the two eldest Owen boys, far away at boarding school in Switzerland. He was friendly with Mr Sheddon's own children and with all the servants inside the house and outside in the garden. They told him again and again how lucky he was to be taken into Mr Owen's house and how far he might go under the butler's teaching.

"The maister's taken a likin to ye, laddie," they all said to him with friendly grins.

On three evenings a week, soon after seven o'clock, Jockie ran down the hill to the school in the Institute where he shared one dog-eared book with fifteen other weary boys and took his turn to read aloud, stumbling slowly over the long words while the others half-listened. The boys were sometimes so tired after their day in the mill that they fell fast asleep, their arms on the desk and their heads on their arms. All around the Big Hall, other groups of boys and girls were reading out loud, turn and turn about, in droning voices. The different stories became muddled in Jockie's mind as he overheard all the readers at once. He only wished he could get his hands on the wonderful book the master had told him about. *Robinson Crusoe*. That sounded like a really good story.

Jockie's first attempts at writing, with the cold slate-pencil gripped tight in his fingers, were awkward, but he was surprised to find how quick he was at arithmetic. Soon he was adding and subtracting and multiplying the numbers with easy confidence, at first on the slate and then in his head. Grown men of all ages sat in the class next door, some of them white-bearded, all of them struggling to remember their letters and to make their figures slowly and carefully on their slates, just like children.

"You seem to have a gift for numbers, lad," said the teacher, delighted with Jockie's grasp of figures, "but you'll need to work much harder at your reading and writing. You're lagging too far behind the others."

In the mill, Henny had now been promoted from the scutching to carding. She worked on one of the big carding engines with a middle-aged man and an elderly woman. They showed her how to feed the broad laps of cotton into the machine, where it was noisily combed and carded into straight fibres by hundreds of sharp needle-points fixed into sheets of leather on a huge roller. The cotton came out of the carder in long, soft slivers, a bit like loose ropes, ready to be stretched and drawn in yet another machine to make rovins for the spinners downstairs.

"Keep both yer ears wide open, Henny, and listen to this wonderful engine of ours," said the old woman,

Annie Sutherland, her back bent crooked from thirty years in the mill. She patted the machine affectionately as she spoke as if it were an enormous pet dog. "Then ye'll be able to hear if somethin's wrong with the cardin, and I'll show ye how to set it right again. Good sharp ears. That's what ye need in this mill. Mine are no as good as they used to be. We all go rather dull o' hearin in the mills, ye ken. From the terrible noise. But Henny, we dinna need to use our ears when we're wantin to have a wee crack and blether while we work. Ye must look at my lips and read the words as I talk. Look at me now, lass, and ye'll get the idea."

Henny turned her face towards Annie's and kept her eyes on the old thin lips that moved with slow and exaggerated movements, shaping each word carefully in turn. At first she was bewildered and had no idea what Annie was saying, but gradually she found she was reading the silent lips as plainly as if she had heard Annie speak.

"Dinna ye be worryin about the mill-fever," Annie said to her in this strange speech one morning. "It's bound to hit ye sometime. All yer family'll have a wee bout of it, except for that lucky laddie up at Braxfield House."

"Whatever is it?" Henny asked in alarm, moving her own lips just as slowly as Annie's.

"Naethin to fash about. Naethin like the smallpox or the cholera. Everyone gets a touch of mill-fever after the first few months in a mill. First ye'll start to feel tired and your head'll ache. Ye'll have a sore throat and stiff arms and legs. Then ye'll no want to eat and yer poor body'll be quiverin from the poundin of the engines. But bit by bit it'll pass and ye'll get used to spendin yer days penned up inside this grand mill with hundreds of ither people and ye'll get used to workin in the heat and noise with the stinkin oil and the smelly privies and the clouds o' cotton flue. Mill-fever disna last lang. Not in Mr Owen's mills. The mills in Dundee are far, far worse."

"But Annie, how could ye possibly ken a thing about fever in the Dundee mills?" Henny asked. "Have ye been there?"

"Na, never, I'm glad to say!" Annie laughed, throwing back her snowy white head. "But we hear plenty about tither mills, all over the country. Some o' the guid folk here used to work in yon awful places, ye see, and they tell us such wicked tales. There was a young laddie came here only last year from an awful mill in Dundee. He'd lost the wee finger off his left hand. Caught it in a machine when he was only eight years old, he told me. That poor bairn was beaten so hard with a thick stick by the overseer in yon Dundee mill that his mither went straight off in fury to seek for the man. She found him at the top of the stairs so she grabbed him with both her hands and she threw him right down to the bottom! Then she had to run awa from the mill takin the lad with her. I dinna ken what became of her, poor woman. Perhaps she deed or went to prison but the bairn walked all the way here from Dundee, though he was only twelve and a wee laddie for his age. He told us such tales of the drunkenness and dirt in yon terrible mill, and about the rats runnin everywhere, and the shockin rude songs the poor women sang as they worked and the cruel maister and the rough overseers, and the lang hours, and the bairns startin work at seven years old, and the ugsome food, and the damp cellars for sleepin. He couldna believe his luck when he came here and Mr Owen gave him work. A kindly family in Long Row offered the lad one end of a bed."

"Is he still here?" asked Henny with interest.

The woman shook her head.

"Na, he was too restless. His faither had been a souter – for mendin broken shoes, ye ken – and the laddie wanted to follow his faither's trade. So he walked off into Perthshire, hopin to find work with a souter. I often think o' him, poor laddie. He told me all about the mill-fever in Dundee. Children lyin sick and shiverin on the floor beside their machines, he said, and naebody to help them. Ye'll never get it as bad as that here, Henny. Just keep on at your work and the fever'll pass. The New Lanark mills are verra hailsome, ye ken. Our maister makes sure o' that."

"Annie Sutherland!" barked the overseer suddenly, right behind her. "Stop all that bletherin and keep yer mind on yer work. I'm settin a bad mark by yer name in the book and yer monitor'll be turned to black the morn! Henny Sinclair, I'm warnin ye. Dinna ye take up Annie's bad habits or yer own monitor'll soon be black!"

Annie Sutherland's lips were still at once. She and Henny turned their eyes obediently back to their shuddering machine. As the long hours passed, Henny's whole body seemed to shake and tremble in time with the carding engine. Her eyes were blurred. Her ears sang in a bewildering fog of noise. She tried to think about the waterfall and the badger in the woods but the clamorous machines dragged her mind back to the mill.

In the day school, Betty could now chant right through the alphabet from A to Z. She sang it like a song, rocking backwards and forwards on her chair. She was learning to march with a straight back and to dance gracefully with the little boys while a fiddler played a set of old Scottish tunes. She knew about the countries where elephants and tigers lived, far over the sea, and she could recite off by heart the names of all the large rivers in Scotland.

Betty seemed happy in the school but something was not quite right. She'd begun to wander off by herself. Almost every day, one or another of the small girls from her class would rush up to the teacher in the schoolyard at playtime, shouting a shrill warning.

"Betty's awa out the gate again, sir!"

It was true every time. Betty had found a clever way of unhooking the latch on the gate in the high wire fence that kept the school children penned safely inside the yard. Once out of the gate, Betty ran for the river, only a little way downstream from the mills. When she reached the river, she sat as good as gold on a flat grey stone and looked out over the turbulent water, rocking backwards and forwards and singing happily to herself.

"Betty! Betty! Come back to the school!" the teacher called urgently every time, hurrying to find her, taking her by the hand, leading her in through the gate again and fixing the latch more firmly. Betty never protested. She was perfectly willing to go with her teacher. She liked him. But she took no notice at all of his stern voice telling her never to lift that latch again and never to wander off alone to the river. Betty just smiled a secret smile of her own and nodded her head obediently. The next day, she was out the gate again and away. Her teacher's patience was wearing thin.

"There's something very strange about that Sinclair lassie," he said to Mr Buchanan one morning. "She must be cured of this wandering off to the river. She needs a good beating!"

"No, no!" Mr Buchanan replied in shocked tones. "You know what the master says. No beatings! Kindness and gentleness! That's the only way to teach!"

The young teacher shook his head in despair but he would not dare to break the master's rules. He would lose his job if he ever struck the girl, so he gritted his teeth and tried yet again to be patient with Betty's daily wanderings. At least she always went to the very same place and never put even one bare toe into the fast-flowing water.

"Tell me, Betty, why do you come here?" the young teacher asked her one day when he found her by the river yet again.

"I just like lookin at the water, sir," she said to him with a smile, "and I like thinkin o' the sea. Yon deep blue sea's aye callin to me, sir."

The teacher sighed at her strangeness and her stubbornness.

By this time, the Sinclairs, like all the other mill families, had completely accepted the master's rule that every day except Sunday had exactly the same regular pattern, strictly marked by the mill's loud clanging bell, from the early morning's awakening, through a fixed order of work, meals and rest to the weary home-coming and the night-school and then the last bell of the long day. The curfew bell. No-one was allowed to be out on the streets after that curfew. No noise of singing or laughing or talking, let alone wild drinking, was to come from the houses. The deep silence of night fell on the village of New Lanark.

Once Henny had grown used to the constant noise in the carding room and to the strain of keeping pace with her machine, she began to look about her with sharp and curious eyes. That was when she began really to notice the visitors. Every day of the working week they came. Even early in September, when the autumn wind began to blow a little colder along the deep Clyde valley, the flood of visitors never stopped. Down the rough winding track from the Old Town they came in their beautiful horse-drawn carriages. Some of them, so Annie Sutherland told Henny in her silent voice, came from Glasgow and Edinburgh, some from Manchester and London, some from America and Germany and Russia. The gentlemen helped the ladies as they stepped down from the carriages in their fine dresses, exclaiming at the well-swept streets, eager to go right inside the mills and to watch the hands at work. Unless he happened to be away on one of his trips to Glasgow or London, Mr Owen himself met his visitors the minute they arrived and conducted them proudly from mill to mill, from nursery to school, talking excitedly all the time as he explained everything they saw. His eyes were always shining with enthusiasm, his lips were always smiling and his flow of talk never ran dry. Henny soon grew used to the astonished questions she could just manage to hear the visitors shouting to him in voices that rose only faintly over the roar of machines. Every day came the same old questions, but the master never seemed to tire of answering them.

"And is it true that you never let the overseers beat your mill-hands, Mr Owen?   Not even for drunkenness or insolence or coming late to work?"

"But Mr Owen, whatever is the use of all that foolish dancing the children do?"

"And shouldn't they be singing the Psalms instead of those quaint old Scottish love-songs, Mr Owen?"

"I've heard you send some of the women from house to house, hunting for fleas and cockroaches, Mr Owen? What a splendid idea! That's just what we need in the slums of Manchester!"

"And is it really true that you don't let the children start work in your mills till they're ten years old, Mr Owen? That seems very late. Why can't they start at six or seven?"

"And why do you make those poor children waste time learning about the wild animals of Africa, Mr Owen? They'll never go to those foreign places, will they?"

Henny loved listening to Mr Owen's patient replies. She thought the words dropped from his mouth like silver pennies. Without pausing in her work, she watched as each group of ladies in their muslins and silks, each group of gentlemen, so confident and charming, finally stepped out of the carding room and went downstairs to watch the spinning on the lower floors. She knew they'd then go back to their waiting carriages. She could imagine them moving slowly up the hill again and perhaps even taking the road through the gate in the high wall, right into the Bonnington estate where she had been with Jockie and Rab. They'd gaze at the waterfall! Corra Linn! She imagined them sitting at their ease in that little house of mirrors, signing their names in the book, sipping their tea from delicate cups and looking up at the terrifying reflections of the falling torrent. In her mind's eye she could see it all.

One morning, to Henny's astonishment, one of the visitors stopped close beside her and spoke.

"Do you enjoy your work on that machine, little girl?" the lady bellowed into her ear.

Henny shook her head.

"Oh yes she does, Madam!" broke in Mr Owen quickly, raising his own voice over the noise. "It's just that this child's still quite new here. Her family only arrived from Caithness in July. It takes my overseers a good six months to get a new family properly broken in to the mill routine. The poor folk keep thinking of their old homes at first, you know, and they're not used to being inside all day. They're often restless to start with and some of them pine for the sea and the open air, but bit by bit they get to love this place and then they never want to leave it. They forget about the sea. They become very fond of their machines too. They even talk to them, so the overseers tell me, and they sing so happily while they work! Now let me take you downstairs, Madam, to see the spinning."

The fine ladies and gentlemen moved away, their hands clapped over their ears to keep out the racket. The lady who had asked Henny the question kept looking back at her with a puzzled frown on her face.

The next party of visitors were all gentlemen from England. None of them stopped to ask Henny if she was happy. They hardly seemed to notice the mill-hands all around them. Their loud braying talk was about some terrifying event a few weeks back, in Manchester. Henny shivered with fear as she heard it.

"Ignorant louts, every one of them!" said one of the gentlemen, angrily. "They flocked to St Peter's Fields in a huge crowd to hear that dangerous fellow, Hunt, shouting for a vote for every man! All nonsense, of course!"

"They were brandishing their sticks, so I've heard," said another. "There could've been a revolution! Just like France!"

"Lucky the cavalry rode in and shot a few of them dead," said a third man. "Teach them a lesson!"

"It's always the same," the first man complained gloomily. "First these foolish mill-hands want shorter hours, then they want higher wages and now they want to vote!"

"It's ridiculous!" laughed another. "If we give in to them, the next thing will be the women wanting to vote!"

"Never! Impossible!" chortled all the gentlemen, rocking back on their heels in mirth as the machines thrummed around them.

"You're right about the vote, sir," Mr Owen said mildly. "No good can come from giving poor men the vote. But those mill-owners in Manchester should come up here to learn a thing or two from me. With shorter hours and fairer treatment, the hands will actually work much harder and spin more cotton. Then the profits will be higher and everyone'll be happier, the owners *and* the workers. There'll never be any protests or revolutions or silly demands for the vote in a peaceful place like New Lanark. My good people here know how lucky they are. I'm like a father to them all. We're a big happy family!"

Henny glanced at Annie Sutherland. Annie winked at her. Mr Owen led his gentlemen towards the door, all of them talking merrily as they went.

"Where's Manchester?" Henny mouthed to Annie.

"Down in England somewhere," said Annie. "It's a big mill-town. I saw it on a map in our school one night. But we dinna need to worry about the strange things that happen down there, Henny. England's anither country, after all."

"Do ye go to the night-school yersel, Annie?" Henny asked her in astonishment, looking at Annie's white hair and the deep lines on her face. She seemed so very old. Far too old for any school.

"Aye, Henny, and I love it! I've learnt the readin in yon school! Now I'm startin on the writin. Ye should tell yer mammie to come along wi' me."

Henny laughed out loud at first. It seemed such a strange idea. But then she was silent. Perhaps her mother really could learn to read one day.

CHAPTER 9

𐄐𐄐𐄐

Trooning the School

New Lanark, late September 1819

"Rab!" Henny called out eagerly, catching sight of him in the street, just at the end of work one day late in September. She hadn't seen Rab for a week or more.

Rab waved and ran towards her.

"What is it?" he asked, his eyes shining at her from under his untidy thatch of hair.

"I'm wantin to sclim round yon wall again," she whispered, glancing over her shoulder to make sure no-one else was listening. "I'm wantin to see yon bonny wood and linns, ye ken. I'm wantin Jockie to come too."

Rab looked puzzled.

"But Henny," he said, "Jockie's awa at the maister's house now. He canna come over the wall any mair."

"He's in the school three nights in the week, Rab. We could easy troon the school. Our mammie will never ken a thing about it."

"But ye'd be far too feart to swing round the end o' yon wall. Ye were feart last time, remember."

"I'm no feart!" Henny said boldly, standing up straight and trying to look more brave than she really felt.

"Tonight then," Rab agreed with a grin. " We'll all troon the school. I only hope my faither disna hear of it."

"He'll never hear!" said Henny. "We'll meet ye by the wall's end." She ran off home for her supper, her heart thumping in excitement and terror.

An hour later, she was waiting by the path up to Braxfield House so she could catch Jockie on his way down to the school. The minute he came into sight, she rushed towards him.

"Jockie! Rab's takin us over yon wall again! We're trooning the school!"

"Now?" Jockie asked her in amazement.

Henny nodded.

"But the dominie'll tell our mammie if we're no there in the class for our readin," he protested.

"The dominie's sick," said Henny. "Some new teacher'll be takin the readin. He disna ken who we are so he'll never notice if we're there or no."

Jockie's face cleared. He leapt up in the air in sheer pleasure at the thought of going over that wall again.

As they skirted around the Institute and ran up by the river to the very end of the wall, Rab himself sprang out of a bush to join them with a shout. Henny stepped right to the edge of the high river-bank and peered cautiously over. The yellow water was roaring beneath her, under its mantle of foam. Her new-found confidence seeped away suddenly and she drew back in fear.

"Come on!" said Rab, never even pausing to ask if she really could face that swing over the river. His fingers were in the two holes and in an instant he was on the far side, laughing out loud at the ease of flying round the end of the wall after all his long years of practice. Jockie followed him without a minute's hesitation, flinging himself boldly into the hidden woods. Henny knew it was now or never. She clutched at the holes. She shut her eyes, leant back over the churning water and moved round the wall. Now she stood safely under the tall trees with Jockie and Rab beside her.

"Look!" she exclaimed in sudden pleasure, her fear dissolving at once. "The leaves are changin colour already. There's yellow and red and brown. And some of them are startin to fall. These woods look different from last time, Rab."

"Are we goin up to the mirror-house first?" Jockie broke in eagerly.

"Na, no just yet," said Rab, leaving the river altogether and turning onto another path under the trees. "I'm wantin to see if there's any brocks about. They dinna play outside so often when the weather turns cooler but we might be lucky. There's still some light in the sky."

Henny and Jockie ran swiftly after Rab. They were so used to a lifetime of bare feet that they didn't feel the stab of rough twigs or the prick of sharp stones. Rab soon found the badgers' narrow pathway through the long grass. They walked carefully beside the path, not brushing against it, until they came right to the mouth of the sett. Then the three of them sat silent on the ground a few paces up the hillside, their backs against a broad oak. They gazed down at the black hole below them, hoping to see a bright eye or a striped face peering out. Nothing happened.

After a fruitless wait of half an hour, Rab got stiffly to his feet with a sigh of disappointment.

"It's nae use at all!" he said. "It's gettin too dark here under the trees. Let's mak for the river. We might see a heron standin on one leg down there, as still as a stane."

As they moved quietly back through the woods, Henny thought she heard a whining and whimpering sound. It seemed very close. She pulled on Rab's arm.

"Listen!" she whispered. Rab stood still.

"What is it?" Jockie asked as the strange noise stopped for a few seconds and then started up again.

"I'm no sure," said Rab, his face puzzled. "It might be some wee creature in trouble. Let's look over this way. Be careful where ye put yer feet. We dinna want to tread on it, whatever it is."

Then all at once they saw him, lying in the shadows. A fully grown badger, caught in a trap, one front paw clamped between the sharp iron teeth, both his back legs scrabbling desperately in the grass. He pulled again and again on the trap but it was pinned firmly to the ground and he couldn't loosen it. He squealed in pain with every jerk, turning his striped face helplessly this way and that, lifting his long nose high in the air.

Henny gasped in horror.

"How did yon cruel gin get there, Rab?" she asked.

"The keeper sets them," said Rab softly, trying to move closer to the badger without frightening him any more. "He has to keep the foxes down, ye ken, to protect his precious game birds. He disna like brocks much either and he disna like moles or weasels or stoats or red squirrels or red kites or eagles. 'Vermin' he calls them. Sometimes he even brings his dogs to dig poor brocks out o' the ground. Then he kills them with a stick."

Henny shuddered.

"What can we do?" she breathed.

"It'll no be easy," said Rab. "A frightened brock can give ye a terrible bad bite with those sharp teeth o' his. First we'll need a strong forked stick."

Rab searched under the trees till he discovered the kind of stick he was looking for and then two more sticks, short and stout. He pulled off his shirt.

"Jockie, ye and Henny take these short sticks. I'll throw my sark over the brock's head to blindfold him so he's no scared to see us. Then I'll pin him down wi' this forked stick at the back o' his neck. That's so he canna bite us. Henny, ye'll press yer ain stick hard against the bottom jaw o' the gin. Push it further into the ground but dinna let yer hands come near his mouth. Jockie, ye'll use yer stick to lift the top jaw up a bit. Then the brock can pull his poor leg out. Right?"

Henny and Jockie nodded. They crouched behind the badger, ready with their sticks. The terrified animal had smelt them now. He was struggling more fiercely, snapping around him wildly with his teeth. In one swift movement, Rab flung his shirt over the badger's head and pulled it tight. Then he pinned him down firmly with the forked stick.

"Quick!" he cried urgently. "Open the jaws!"

Henny pressed her stick harder and harder on the lower teeth of the gin. Jockie levered his stick under the top jaw. The rusty old jaws were stiff and strong.

"I canna move it!" Jockie cried out in despair as the badger kept scraping violently with his back legs and heaving his whole body against Rab's forked stick.

"Wheesht! Keep yer voice low and try again," gasped Rab, leaning his weight on the badger's back and almost sitting on him. The animal's breath came faster in frantic moans and gasps.

"Ow!" shrieked Henny suddenly, dropping her stick altogether. "He's bitten me through yer sark, Rab. My hand's bleedin!"

"Pick up yer stick and try again," Rab said calmly. "A wee bite canna hurt ye, Henny! A fisherman's lassie's aye brave and strong!"

Henny remembered her father. Rab was right. She grabbed the fallen stick and pressed harder still on the lower jaw of the trap, not bothering about the blood that ran over her fingers and dripped all over Rab's shirt and down to the ground. Jockie pushed his own stick under the top jaw again and strained it upwards. Slowly, very slowly, he managed to prise the rusty teeth open just a little.

The badger snatched his paw away, blood pouring from the deep wound. With a sudden leap he was gone, limping badly as he ran, shaking Rab's sark from his head and disappearing under the trees.

"Will he get better?" Jockie asked anxiously, releasing the trap with a loud snap as soon as Henny's stick and hands were well out of the way.

"I'm no sure," said Rab, retrieving his torn shirt, all smeared with blood, and quickly pulling it on again. "He'll lie low in his sett for a week or two. He might get better. He might dee."

There was a long silence.

"I want to gang back to the mills, Rab," Henny said quietly. "My hand's still bleedin. It's throbbin."

"The woods are scarey!" said Jockie, shivering all of a sudden and looking all around him in the thickening twilight.

"We'll tie up that bite first, Henny," said Rab, producing a grubby handkerchief from his pocket. "We'll stop the bleedin. When we get to the mill-lade, we'll wash it clean."

Henny nodded. The bite was hurting her even more now but she blinked back the tears as Rab tied the handkerchief tightly.

"Hame!" she begged him.

"But do ye no want to look for the heron first?" Rab asked her, surprised and disappointed. "Do ye no want to see the keekin-glasses in the wee house again? And Corra Linn, the bonny waterfall?"

Jockie and Henny shook their heads. They had seen quite enough for one night.

As they turned for home, an angry dog barked somewhere close behind them. A hidden pocket-watch chimed its silver chime. A man's voice called out roughly.

"Who's there? Stay where ye are! Ye canna get awa!"

"The keeper!" hissed Rab. "He's checkin his traps. Run for the wall!"

Their feet flew over the grass. Rab knew the way well, dodging trees, leaping where no paths had ever been, hurtling straight down the hill to the river. Henny and Jockie followed in his footsteps, gasping for breath as they ran. They could hear the keeper and his dog blundering about under the trees. The man was cursing.

"Dratted mill children," he muttered, his pace slowing a little. "Trespassin in my woods and takin all the nuts from my trees, nae doubt! I'll grab them next time! I'll drag them to the maister!"

At the end of the long wall Rab and Jockie and Henny swung themselves out over the river and back to safety without even a second's pause to look down at the turbulent water below. They didn't stop running till they reached the mills, leaning against the great stone buildings to catch their breath.

"We'll . . . we'll . . . never be able to wander in yon woods again!" Jockie said, choking back a sob.

"Och aye, we will, Jockie!" Henny said, surprising even herself. Her heart was still beating wildly with fear.

"There's plenty ither fine places where we could go," said Rab. "Like down the river to Stanebyres Linn."

"I dinna want the ither places," said Henny. "I want to see that poor brock again. To find if his leg gets better."

"We'll see," Rab said cautiously. "The gloamin comes down sooner in October. Yon Bonnington keeper disna like the dark and the cold, as I've told ye, so he'll stay all night in his house. We'd need a bit of a moon, ye ken, or we'd never see a thing."

"Good!" breathed Henny, smiling to herself as her courage flooded back again.

"We'll dip yer sore hand in the mill-lade, Henny," Rab said, leading her to a place where she could lie flat beside a fast-flowing stream and trail her bitten hand in the cold water till the bleeding really had stopped and the pain had eased a little.

"When ye get home, tie a clean bandage round it," said Rab. "Tie it firm and tight!"

"Yer as good as a doctor, Rab," laughed Henny.

"But dinna let yer mither see yon bite," Rab warned her, "or she'll be askin questions. Keep yer hand behind yer back or deep in yer pocket."

Henny nodded.

It was far too late to go into school now but far too soon to go home. All the reading classes were still droning away in their different rooms in the Institute as Rab took Henny and Jockie tiptoeing quietly past the mills to the point where he always followed his own track up to the Old Town and Jockie his path to Braxfield House.

"We'll sit here under the bushes till the school's ended,"

Rab whispered, wriggling into a safely hidden place under a curtain of low-hanging autumn leaves.

"Rab!" Henny suddenly whispered back at him, remembering those visitors at the mill. "Have ye ever heard of a terrible battle on St Peter's Fields?"

Rab gasped.

"I have!" he murmured. "My faither's aye talkin of it, day and night! Peterloo, he calls that battle. Waterloo was a grand victory but Peterloo in Manchester was a shameful thing, my faither says. But who told ye about the killin on St Peter's Fields, Henny? The mill-folk here in New Lanark wouldna ken a thing about yon terrible day."

"Na, it wasna the mill-folk that told me. It was some o' the maister's fine gentlemen, comin to see the mills. I heard them talkin. But Rab, the gentlemen didna think it was a terrible day at all! They said it was a grand day. Some wicked men were killed, they said, and the one called Hunt was put in prison. They said we must keep them down or we'll have a revolution. Like yon poor people over the sea in France!"

"Ye've been listenin to a lot o' wicked blethers, Henny," Rab said, almost fiercely. "It was cruel what yon sodgers on their horses did at St Peter's Fields. The mill-hands had no weapons but the sticks in their hands but the sodgers mowed them down, shootin and slashin at them. Blood everywhere! Screamin and groanin! A massacre, that's what my faither says it was! We lost that battle of Peterloo, Henny, but we'll win the next one!"

Henny was surprised. It all sounded so different from the victory over a wild rabble that the fine gentlemen had been talking about. Could it really be the same Peterloo, she wondered, or was Rab mixing it all up with something else? She was just about to ask him when he suddenly seemed to tire of talking with her about the tragic battle down south in Manchester. He turned his head quickly away and started to whistle quietly to himself, hiding himself still lower under the bushes.

"What's that tune, Rab?" Henny asked him.

"I've heard you whistle it before," Jockie put in. "I like it."

"It's one of my faither's old songs," Rab said, recovering his good temper in a flash. "He heard it when he was only a lad. Robert Burns hissel sang it to him, or so he says! My faither takes care no to sing it doun here by the mills but he aye sings it at hame on a Saturday night when he's had a few drams o' whisky. My grannie isna verra fond o' yon tune but she canna stop my faither singin it!"

"Does it have a name?" Henny asked him.

"Two names," Rab laughed. "Some days my faither calls it the Tree o' Liberty and ither days it's The Tree o' France."

"Are there any words at all, Rab, or is it just a wee tune?" Jockie whispered, leaning still closer.

"There's words all right, and I ken every one o' them," Rab said with a laugh in his voice as if he were guarding a wonderful secret. "But I canna sing them here. We're too near the mills. Anybody on the path might hear me and then there'd be trouble. Come awa up the hill and I'll sing ye a couple o' verses."

Rab charged up the steep path a little way towards the Old Town with new energy. He stopped suddenly by a young tree and stood with his back pressed against it. Jockie and Henny came one each side of him and listened intently. Rab sang his song softly but every word was as clear as a bell.

Heard ye o' the Tree o' France,
And wat ye what's the name o't?
Around it all the patriots dance –
Weel Europe kens the fame o't.

Upon this tree there grows sic fruit,
Its virtue all can tell, man;
It raises man above the brute,
It maks him ken hissel, man.

With plenty o' sic trees, I trow,
The world would live in peace, man;
The sword would help to mak a plough,
The din o' war would cease, man.

Henny was disappointed. The song didn't make much sense to her.

"What dis it mean, Rab?" she asked. "And what's a patriot? I've never heard o' such a word."

"A patriot's somebody who loves his ain country," said Rab, proudly. "My faither told me."

"But everybody dis that!" Jockie protested.

"There's different ways o' lovin yer ain country," Rab explained patiently, dropping his voice lower now. "In

France they had a bloody revolution to win their liberty. Maybe we'll have to do the same here some day soon."

"Na!" Henny said, quite shocked. "People'd get killed!"

Rab only laughed.

"But Rab," Jockie persisted. "What exactly is the Tree o' France? Have ye ever seen it?"

"There's mair than one o' them," Rab whispered, his voice breaking in excitement. "They're planted all over France. All over Germany too and in plenty ither countries. There's even some o' them been planted right here in Scotland, back in the great French Revolution time, and they've grown tall and straight since then. But they're secret trees, ye ken, Jockie. They dinna have a notice pinned on them, saying 'Tree o' Liberty' or 'Tree o' France'. A few brave folk ken fine the places where they're growin and they go to look at them now and then. They like to dance round yon trees when the moon's at the full. Just to remind theirsels o' liberty. My faither showed me one o' yon trees. It's no far from Lanark."

"Liberty, Rab?" Henny demanded in astonishment. "What are ye sayin? We've got our liberty already. We're as free as the birds!"

"Not true liberty, my faither says. One day we'll be really free. Then the poor men'll be able to vote as well as the rich men. There'll be nae mair hungry beggars livin in hedges or cellars, and nae mair wee bairns slavin in the mills. We'll break free from England, when that grand day comes, Henny! We'll own the maister's mills oursels and we'll walk through yon gate in the wall, right into the Bonnington woods. The keeper willna chase us out then!"

Henny laughed, rather too loudly. "You're naethin but a wild dreamer, Rab Cunningham!"

"Wheesht!" whispered Rab. "I'm awa hame up the hill before I gab too much."

And with that he was gone, climbing the steep pathway to the Old Town and whistling his tune cheerfully as he disappeared under the trees. Henny and Jockie turned slowly round to walk down to the mills again and to the clean and orderly peace of New Lanark village.

"We are as free as the birds, Jockie, whatever Rab says!" Henny whispered to him just as he was ready to turn up to Braxfield House.

"I'm no so sure!" Jockie whispered back and then he was gone.

CHAPTER 10

The Pull of Water

New Lanark, October 1819

October had come to New Lanark. White mists hung low over the river until late morning when the bright autumn sunshine broke through at last and the mills emerged slowly from the vapour like ships from fog at sea. A sharp wind blew red and yellow leaves from the trees high over the village and from the hidden woods beyond the wall. The scavengers were busier than ever in the streets, gathering the leaves into restless piles, chasing after them with their birch-twig besoms, shovelling them onto horse-drawn carts and carrying them away to make sweet-smelling compost for the Clydesdale farms.

Now it was lighting-up time at the mills. The overseers ordered twenty of the older boys to get out of bed in the dark at five o'clock every morning to light the oil lamps in every mill, to set them safely on every shelf and to hang them high over every machine. Their next job was to stoke up the huge iron stoves that were built into the end wall of each of the mills. They threw great lumps of coal into the blazing stoves so that warm air flowed up metal ducts to the higher floors, to keep the workers warm and the cotton easy to handle. Then the boys rushed on to the Institute, lighting the school lamps and pitching coal into the furnace to send heat to every classroom. When the morning bell began to ring and the hundreds of mill-hands came running through the dark streets to get to their work on time, New Lanark was glowing with light.

Henny stopped in astonishment as she stepped into her mill. The whole place looked utterly different. Yellow lamps shone down on the rows of shadowy machines, shedding pools of light onto rollers and wheels, spindles and belts, and onto the flickering lines of white cotton yarn. The grim water-frames seemed almost beautiful in the lamplight.

"Hurry along there, Henny Sinclair!" the overseer called sharply. "Run up the stairs, ye foolish lass."

Henny ran. By the end of her first hour, the mill was almost too hot from the burning stoves and the smoking lanterns. The smell of warm oil made her feel sick. She swayed dizzily on her feet as the carding engines shuddered and clattered. Her hands trembled. She longed for the nine o'clock break and for the comforting taste of porridge in her mouth.

Meanwhile, Betty was still playing happily in the enclosed yard outside the Institute, filling in time with games until school began. She held one end of a long, heavy rope. Her friend, Ishbel, held the other end. They turned the rope in a steady rhythm as the other girls ran in, skipped for a while, and then ran out again. At half past seven exactly, the school bell rang for classes to start. Betty dropped her end of the rope at once and moved off obediently with the other children towards the door where they lined up in pairs, waiting for the command to march briskly into the classrooms like a tiny army. She took her place at a long desk beside four other eight-year olds. Carefully she copied letters of the alphabet onto her slate, humming quietly to herself.

"Betty Sinclair!" her teacher snapped. "What's that singing noise I can hear?"

Betty smiled up at him.

"It's one of our old songs from Wick, sir. The fishermen are aye singin it when they're pullin up the sails. It tells the story of a mermaid, sir."

"A mermaid!" the teacher laughed. "You should be forgetting all about mermaids and such like by now, Betty. The sea's a very long way from here. Keep your mind on your lessons and don't think about mermaids! This is not the singing time, you know. This is the writing time. Do you hear me?"

Betty nodded. Her face was sad. She bent her head down so low over her slate that her hair became tangled

130

with her pencil. In silence she copied her letters, one after another, until the first shafts of daylight began to filter down from the high windows. Now two boys were sent to snuff out the early lamps and to stack them carefully in cupboards. Slate-pencils squeaked on slates. The unpleasant smell of all the small wet rags, used for cleaning the slates, filled the schoolroom. From the room next door came the sound of older children chanting the seven-times table. Betty felt drowsy. Her mind kept drifting back to mermaids and the sea. She even thought she could hear the green waves breaking on the sands at Wick. At last the breakfast bell rang out from the mills.

"Get ready to march out properly, children!" the teacher said sharply. "No rushing!"

The girls and boys formed up into a long line, two by two. They stood with shoulders back and heads held high. The fife band struck up a tune. The boy on the drum rapped his sticks.

"Quick march!" cried the teacher. The girls and boys in Betty's class strode briskly out of the classroom and across the playground to the open gate. Then they dashed for their homes.

Betty was the last to leave. She hesitated for a moment outside the gate. Then, instead of turning towards Caithness Row and her family's warm room and her bowl of porridge, she turned the other way, though she hardly knew why. Something seemed to be pulling her. She began to run, flying past the four mills on light feet till the cobbled street ended. Then she sped down a muddy path until she reached her flat stone by the river's edge. She sat on the stone, shivering a little in the cold air and gazing across the water at a long-legged heron that flapped slowly upwards through the mist. She felt happy.

"Are ye no goin hame for yer breakfast, lassie?" a friendly voice asked close behind her.

Betty turned her head. A boy stood there. A big boy as old as Henny. His face was broad and his brown hair was smooth. He fixed his pale eyes on Betty and smiled down at her.

"What are ye doin here by the river, lassie?" he asked her pleasantly. "Should ye no be back in yer ain house, eatin up yer mammie's porridge?"

"I'll be goin hame soon," she said, returning his smile. "I was just wantin to watch the river. I like sittin here an listenin to the rushin noise o' the brown water. It maks me think o' the sea."

"The sea?" he asked, puzzled.

"Aye, the sea at Wick in Caithness.'

"Wick! Ye're no one o' yon Sinclair family, are ye?" The boy sounded suddenly eager.

Betty nodded, happy that he'd heard of them.

"Aye," she said. "I'm Betty. We came here in July."

"And how do ye like our maister's fine mills, Betty?" he asked her.

"No much," she said honestly. "They're naethin like the sands at Wick and there's nae sea here at all. But I like the good food we're eatin and I like our big new room in Caithness Row and I like the lassies in the school. The schoolroom smells awful strange this mornin. My head keeps whirlin."

The boy nodded.

"That's the smell o' the lamps, Betty. Ye'll soon get used to it. I'm used to it. I was born here, ye ken. I've never seen the sea."

"Never seen the sea!" Betty cried out in pity for this poor boy, whoever he was.

"There's better things here than the sea," he said. "There's otters in yon river."

"Otters?" Betty was excited now. "Where?" She turned her eyes back to the rushing river, hoping to catch sight of a sleek black head in the water.

"There's an otter's holt someplace near here," the boy said, suddenly flinging himself down onto her flat stone and hanging well out over the water. "I'll soon show ye, Betty. It's just a wee hole in the bank where the otters live."

The boy held fast with one hand to the root of a tree and poked about right under the bank with his other hand, searching for an entrance to the otter's home.

"Here it is!" he cried in triumph. "Look!"

He scooped up a handful of pebbles and flung them hard into a black hole just above the water-line.

Betty stretched out beside the kind boy and leant cautiously forward. She glimpsed the hole for one excited instant and then pulled quickly back again.

"I canna see the otters," she said, disappointed.

"They're verra shy and quick," explained the boy. "They whistle, ye ken. Ye'll hear them whistlin before ye see them. I ken how to whistle them right out o' their holes. The silly beasts think it's anither otter callin. I'll just try whistlin now and ye keep yer eyes on yon hole."

Betty gazed obediently down at the hole. She leant her head out as far as she dared, watching intently for an otter. The boy began to whistle. A soft, uncanny tune. Betty listened. At that very moment she felt a pair of rough hands grasping her two bare feet from behind. She seemed to be tipping forward. Or was she floating on the air? Or flying like a heron? Was this some new kind of game? Whatever it was, she couldn't stop herself. She let out a wild shriek of fear, calling to the kind boy to help her. She snatched at the bank but her fingers slipped on mud. She hit the water with a splash. Her head went under. She swallowed a mouthful and came up again, coughing and spluttering, gasping for air. Her arms thrashed wildly. The powerful brown current tossed her onto her back as it swept her helplessly downstream, her cotton tunic full of air, buoying her up, her arms and legs scraping against jagged rocks. She caught one misty glimpse of the friendly boy running back towards the mills and then the river carried her away.

"Help! Help!" Betty called but there was no-one to hear her. Now the rough water began to roll her over and over. She struggled to breathe each time her face came up into the light but her strength was going fast. She struck out blindly with her hands, lunging towards the bank with her whole body, but the struggle was hopeless. The strong river that turned the mills' great wheels held her firmly in its grip. It tossed her like flotsam out into mid-stream and then hurled her far over towards the other side.

At the first wide bend, Betty was flung hard, face forward, against a dead tree that lay half-submerged in the water. Instantly her head and shoulders were wedged between a sloping branch and the tree-trunk, her mouth only a few inches above the churning yellow foam. Her legs and feet dangled helplessly behind her in the river, pushed and pulled this way and that by the current. Gasping and shivering, she scrabbled desperately at the gnarled tree-trunk. Her grip held firm, green slime under her fingernails, but she couldn't pull herself any further up to safety. She was trapped. She called out one last time, her voice faint and full of terror. Then she dropped her head onto her hands. A sudden cold darkness came down. The river poured over her trailing legs. A skein of geese flew high overhead, honking softly in the autumn mist, but Betty did not hear them.

CHAPTER 11

River

New Lanark, October 1819

"Where's Betty?" Christina asked suddenly, pausing in surprise as she dished up the breakfast porridge for her family. "Did she no run back here with ye when the school ended, Tam? Whatever's keepin her?"

Tam shrugged his shoulders and began eating.

"Maybe she's gone hame with her friend, Ishbel," Henny suggested with a laugh. "Porridge aye tastes better in anither lassie's house."

"She'd no go off with anither lassie unless she asked me first," her mother protested. "Betty's such a good wee bairn. I've told her no to wander off from the school and she's promised me."

Davie started to cry, rubbing his eyes with grubby hands. Christina turned to help him, spooning the porridge into his open mouth till the crying stopped.

"Eat up yer own porridge, Mammie," Henny said, scraping her empty dish and licking her lips. "I'll run back to the school and find Betty. She's sure to be there, playin some game or singin some song to hersel! She's aye singin."

"Ask at Ishbel's house if she's no in the schoolroom," her mother said, beginning to think that perhaps Betty might be with her friend after all.

Henny ran to the school first. The high gate was shut but she easily used Betty's own trick of lifting the wire latch. The playground was deserted. She walked right into the building. Every room in the school was empty. Even the teachers had all gone home for their breakfast. Henny rushed from room to room, calling Betty's name until it echoed back from the high walls. She peered under every row of desks and even stared up at the strange wild animals in the Big Hall, as if they might be able to tell her where Betty had gone. Then she hurried on to Ishbel's house but Betty was not there either. Ishbel had not seen her since they'd left the schoolroom together. Henny trudged home again. Until this moment she had not really been worried, but now a sense of panic started to rise in her throat. Her mouth tasted dry with fear.

"I canna find her, Mammie!" she cried, bursting in at the door again.

"River!" squealed Tam, his eyes opening wide in fear.

"What do ye mean, Tam?" his mother asked him.

"River!" Tam repeated just as the mill-bell rang for work to start again.

Christina's face was white. She thrust Davie into Henny's arms, grabbed Tam by the hand and they all ran for the stairs. As they joined the crowds hurrying back to the school and the mills, Christina was shouting out loud to anyone who would listen.

"Our Betty's awa! We canna find her! Did ye no see her? Betty! Betty!"

She paused only to push Tam and Davie safely inside the playground. Then she ran on to the mills with Henny close behind her, both of them still calling for Betty. Now the other women took up their cry. The whole street was ringing with Betty's name.

Willie Grant, the overseer, stood bristling with irritation at the door of his mill, hands on hips.

"What's the trouble?" he demanded crossly. "It's time all ye women were back to work. Wheesht now! Stop that howlin, Christina Sinclair! Ye're upsettin my whole mill!"

"Our Betty's lost!" Christina cried. "I'm awa to the river to find her! Help me!"

The overseer stood speechless as the women pounded over the cobbles behind Christina and Henny, all heading downstream for the river. He made to grab one or two of them to hold them back but they pulled away from his hands and ran on.

"Betty! Betty!" they cried as the bell stopped ringing.

"The maister'll hear of this!" the overseer bawled

after them. "There's to be no missin work without permission! Ye ken the rules! Ye'll be fined a shillin, every one of ye!"

Just at that moment Rab came out of Number Four Mill with his father, John Cunningham, a tall, thin man with red hair and a straggly red beard. They stopped in astonishment as they caught the sound of Willie Grant's angry voice and then the wild cry of the running women.

"What's happenin?" Rab shouted to an elderly woman who was tottering past him on stiff legs, trying to catch up with the screaming crowd.

"Child lost!" she called. "Betty Sinclair! She's awa to the river!"

"Faither! It's the Sinclair family in trouble. The new folk from Wick!"

Rab dashed down the street with his father beside him. They passed the old woman and pushed on through the crowd and right down the path by the river until they caught up with Christina herself. She was standing with both her bare feet on the flat rock by the edge of the water. Henny stood close, gripping her mother's hand. They were staring out at the river.

"Oh Rab!" Christina cried, catching sight of him. Tears were pouring down her face. "I said she must never come to sit on this cold stane any mair. I said she must never wander by the river. But where else can she be? Henny's searched the school!"

"This is my faither!" Rab gasped, catching his breath. He was alarmed to see her tears. "He's sure to find Betty for ye. Dinna greet!"

But Rab's father looked serious. He spoke gently to Christina.

"If the lassie's fallen into the river, Missus, she could be swept as far down as Stanebyres Falls. Then there's nae hope for her. Many a good man's been lost over yon falls! The pool's so deep, ye ken, and it aye whirls round and round."

Christina gave a cry of despair. Rab's father gripped her arm. Together they peered into the mist that still hung over the river.

"Where's the boat?" shouted Henny. "In Wick we aye run for the boats when anybody's in trouble in the sea."

John Cunningham shook his head.

"Naebody can row against this awful swirl," he said grimly. "The maister disna allow any boats. Too dangerous. Our only hope is that the daft lassie's managed to swim to the bank."

"She canna swim!" cried Henny in horror, her eyes on the swirling water, fearful of seeing a bundle of wet clothes bobbing helplessly about in the current.

Just then, the mist began to lift a little, over the big bend. As the yellow trees on the far side came shimmering into sight, it was Henny who first caught sight of the little figure, wedged in the fork of a fallen tree, well downstream from the rock where they stood.

"Mammie! Look!" she cried, pointing.

"Betty!" all the women shouted together in one new breath of hope.

But, as far as anyone could see at such a distance, Betty made no movement at all. She seemed to be completely

140

still except for her limp legs swaying in the current.

"She canna hear us!" said Henny.

"She must be drouned!" Christina sobbed in despair.

"Maybe not," said John Cunningham. "I think her head's just out o' the water. Dinna give up hope yet, Missus. We canna get across the river from here. We'll tak the scavenger's cart and horse and drive up through the Old Toun and down to the bridge near Kirkfieldbank. Then we'll come upriver again on tither side. It'll tak us a good lang while."

"Can ye no wade straight through the water?" gasped Henny, horrified at such a delay.

John Cunningham shook his head.

"Nae man can do that," he said. "The river's too strong."

"Then how will ye reach her when ye come to tither side?" Henny demanded.

"She's no verra far from yon bank. Rab, ye get me a rope and a saw from the joiners' shop in Number Four. Ye'd better come with me in the cart, lad."

"Me too!" cried Henny. "Betty'll be needin somebody from her ain family."

Rab's father hesitated for a moment but then he nodded. He turned to Christina.

"Missus, ye stay here on the flat stane. Keep gollerin out loud to the poor wee lass. If she's still livin, it's her mither's voice she'll be wantin to hear."

John Cunningham hurried back towards the village and took charge of an empty cart. A horse stood waiting patiently between the shafts. Rab climbed into the cart with his rope, his saw and a knife from the joiners' shop. Henny ran for towels and blankets. Willie Grant sent three men from the mill to join them and then hustled all the women back to their work again.

The cart smelt not of foul dung, as Henny had expected, but of sweet autumn leaves. She was surprised. She sat at the back of the cart on her pile of blankets and towels, listening to the men as they talked mournfully together about all the children they'd ever known who'd been drowned in that river. The horse plodded slowly up the road to the Old Town, steering clear of the heavy wagons that were grinding down to the mills, their carters shouting out cheerfully as they flicked their long whips.

"How can they be so happy," Henny wondered miserably to herself, "when our Betty's stuck in the river?" Her confused thoughts ran round and round in her head. The horse trotted through the crowded streets of Lanark and then started with cautious hoofs on the long road down to the bridge. If only her father had been here! He would have got across that river somehow. He'd never been scared of fast-running water like these poor southern folk. But then she remembered. The wild sea-water had got him in the end. Perhaps these mill-hands were right to be scared.

Now the horse was over the narrow bridge and had turned left onto the muddy track that kept close to the river's edge on the far side.

"Betty!"

Henny cried out the minute she spotted the half-sunken tree. There was the little girl's small dark head pressed against the wet trunk, her shoulders still gripped in the angle of a branch. Henny stood up in the cart, waving and shouting. Her mother shouted faintly back from the other side, her distant body like a black stick, stiff and tense with fear.

"Wheesht, lassie!" said John Cunningham. "Dinna go scarin this old horse with yer shoutin or he'll gallop awa with us! The minute we stop ye must get busy makin a soft bed for yer sister in the back o' the cart here. Pull some bracken to pile up under yon blankets. We'll soon bring Betty out o' the water but ye're the one that must make her warm again. Unless she's deid, o' course. Unless she's deid."

The mist had completely lifted now. The sun shone on the sparkling river. The horse stopped. Rab ran to the water's edge. He tied one end of the rope to a tree and handed the other end to his father together with the saw. Henny set about gathering bracken and leaves for a bed, keeping half an eye always on Betty.

The four men stepped straight into the water, not even pausing to take off their clothes. They moved forwards, one behind the other, each with a turn of the rope around his waist, paying it out steadily from the coils by the tree. Their feet slipped on wet stones. Their arms shot out suddenly to keep their balance as they staggered and floundered in the water. Rab's father always held the saw high in his right hand. The yellow current buffeted and pummelled their legs but somehow they managed to keep their footing. Inch by careful inch they edged closer to

Betty. The water rose to their knees and then to their thighs.

John Cunningham was the first to touch the tree. He put his broad left hand on Betty's back. He pulled and shoved and tugged but he couldn't move her. The second man joined him and then the others. Together they pushed and pulled but Betty didn't budge an inch. So John wielded his saw, slicing carefully through the branch that held her, near to the trunk and as close to her thin body as he dared. He was through! She was free! John Cunningham hoisted the unconscious girl up to his shoulder. Henny heard her mother's cry of joy from the far bank. With the other men pressing close to keep him from falling, he carried Betty carefully to the bank. Henny had only one question.

"Is she deid?"

John Cunningham shook his head.

"I dinna ken yet, Henny lass. She's as cold as death, poor thing. First we'll tip the water out o' her lungs."

He grasped Betty by both her heels and lifted her high in the air with her head towards the ground. A stream of green water flowed out of her mouth. Henny gasped at this rough handling, but worse was to come.

"Good," said John Cunningham when he could shake not even one more drop out of her lungs. "Now we'll swing her like a sickly new-born puppy. Sometimes it gets the breathin goin and the heart pumpin again. Out o' the way there, all of ye!"

Still holding Betty by the ankles he swung her round and round in circles.

144

"Stop!" protested Henny.

John Cunningham took no notice until he was ready. At last he lowered Betty gently to the ground.

"Now ye must keep on speakin to her, Henny, as loud as ye can, while I cut off these wet clothes and rub her dry. Rab, bring the knife and the towels. Be quick!"

"Betty! Betty! Wake up!" Henny called to her sister again and again but the white face was still. The eyes were closed.

Rab laid his ear close against Betty's chest.

"She's breathin, faither!" he cried. "I can hear the air strugglin in and out o' her lungs. It's a kind of gurglin sound."

"I'll lift her onto the cart then," said his father. "We'll roll her into those blankets and we'll hurry her back to the mill. Henny, we'll have to roll ye in the blankets with her. Press yersel close against her and keep on rubbin her hands. That's the way! Yer body might make her warm again. And keep on talkin to her, Henny. All the way home. I'll mak that old horse move faster than he's ever moved before!"

The horse broke into a crazy gallop and the cart lurched back along the track towards the bridge. John Cunningham started to whistle, a rousing kind of tune full of vigour and hope. Henny recognized it at once as she lay close against Betty in the bundle of blankets, trying to make her own warmth seep into that cold, still body. She kept singing the cheerful tune, crooning it over and over again into Betty's ear, as the air came rasping in and out of those river-soaked lungs, stronger and louder with every breath.

Heard ye o' the Tree o' France,
And wat ye what's the name o't?
Around it all the patriots dance –
Weel Europe kens the fame o't.

"Henny?" came a puzzled little voice from the bundle of blankets.

Henny let out a shriek of joy. Betty had spoken! Her eyes were open! She was gazing at Henny in bewilderment as the cart rattled and banged its way home to the mill, shaking every bone in their bodies in spite of the soft pile of bracken. Rab and the men on the cart cheered in relief. John Cunningham urged the horse faster down the last hill to New Lanark.

"I'm awful cold, Henny," said the faint voice from the blankets. "I wish ye'd stop that singin. Yer singin's makin me cold!"

Henny laughed out loud. She hugged Betty tight.

"It's no my singin that maks ye cold, Betty," she said. "It was the river that chilled ye to the bane. Ye fell in the river! Do ye no remember?"

Betty shook her head.

"The big boy was so kind," she murmured.

"What big boy?" Henny asked her in surprise.

Betty sighed and shivered.

"I dinna ken. He said he'd show me an otter. I remember that fine."

"Henny!" John Cunningham called sharply over his shoulder. "Stop pesterin the lassie wi yer daft questions. She's likely forgotten the whole thing. That's all for the best. Just let her be!"

Henny was disappointed. She wanted to know so much more. Who was the kind boy? Had Betty really seen an otter? And how had she slipped into the river? But Henny was silent at once, no longer probing the girl's muddled memories and no longer even singing Rab's rousing song about the Tree of France. She was just thankful to feel the new surge of warmth creeping slowly along Betty's arms and across her chest and down her legs. Betty was alive! That was all that mattered.

When they came at last to New Lanark, deep in its valley, a huge crowd was standing out in the street, waiting in anxious silence. Henny had no idea how they came to be there. It couldn't be time for the dinner-break yet. No bell could have rung so early. The master certainly wouldn't like it if he knew. But there they all were, men, women and children, yelling wildly and laughing and cheering as Henny propped Betty up in the cart for everyone to see her, still swathed in the blankets. Feeble but smiling, Betty waved back to the jubilant crowd like a queen from her carriage, her white cheeks flushed with pink.

CHAPTER 12

Magician

New Lanark, October–November 1819

As John Cunningham carried Betty upstairs to the room in Caithness Row, Rab and Henny pressed close behind him. He lowered the little girl gently onto the bed that Christina had been warming with a large river-stone, heated in a pot of boiling water.

"Let her sleep now," said the surgeon who came straight away to look at Betty. "Don't make her eat till she asks for food. Sleep is the best healer. You can stay here with her for the rest of the day, Christina Sinclair, but your older girl must go straight back to her work. Yes, off you go at once, Henny. And you too, Rab

Cunningham. This is not a holiday, you know. This is a normal working day and the master won't be pleased if he finds everything at sixes and sevens in his mills when he gets home from Glasgow this afternoon. The overseers are having quite enough trouble herding all those foolish hands inside again. Goodness knows what a tangle they'll find when they get back to their spinning. They never should have left their work! It was sheer madness and the master must be told."

The excitement was over in the mills but there was a smile of relief on every face as the hands settled back to their spinning or carding without a murmur, quickly taking up the rhythm of their machines, slipping into the automatic routine that each of them knew so well. The overseers strode grimly about, turning every monitor to black and announcing steep fines for every mill-hand, but for once no-one seemed to care. Betty Sinclair was safe. That was all that mattered.

To the irritation of his overseers, Mr Owen cancelled the fines as soon as he heard the whole story late that afternoon, but he was very worried all the same. That Sinclair family from Wick were always having such unexpected accidents! He began to wonder if he'd been wise to take them on at his mills. First their father had been drowned at sea – though he couldn't help that, poor man. Then Jockie had been hit on the head in the coal-house – not his fault of course. And now this disobedient little girl, Betty, had fallen into the river, all because she'd wandered off by herself instead of going straight home from school to her breakfast. Any more problems with those Sinclairs and he'd have to send them all back to Caithness or they'd make the other workers restless. One bad apple in the barrel could easily turn the whole lot rotten.

Even after a splendid dinner that evening and a glass or two of good red wine, Mr Owen was still plunged in gloom. He kept sighing in irritation and disappointment as he sat with his wife beside a warm fire in the drawing-room at Braxfield House. He simply couldn't stop thinking about those worrying Sinclairs. They had seemed such a promising family when he'd seen them first. Honest too. He'd liked them. But he couldn't close his eyes to this latest terrible accident. That silly girl, Betty, must have gone where she shouldn't have gone or she never would have slipped into the river. Was Rab Cunningham far too friendly with the Sinclair family? He was a bright lad and a good worker but perhaps he'd already been infected by some of his father's dangerous ideas. Rab Cunningham could well be leading those poor Sinclairs astray.

Mr Owen shook his head impatiently and pushed the Sinclair family right out of his mind. He began to think instead about a wonderful new plan for changing the whole country by the simple use of spades instead of ploughs. Work for everyone! No more hunger!

"Robert, my dear, you're dreaming again!" said his wife gently. Robert Owen smiled back at her. His eyes were shining with enthusiasm.

Betty's strength had returned steadily in the warmth of her family's room. First she sat out of bed in a chair with a blanket over her knees. Then she could walk about in her nightshirt, touching the familiar things and humming old songs to herself. Then she was dressed in a clean set of clothes and impatient to go back to school.

"Next week," said her mother, firmly. "Ye're no quite ready yet."

"But, Mammie, I want to go to the concert in the Big Hall on Saturday night! There's a famous warlock comin from Glesca and he'll be castin his magic spells. I canna miss the warlock! And then there'll be the singin. Please Mammie!"

"He's just a conjurer, Betty," her mother laughed. "The maister calls him the magician. He's no a real warlock. He only shows off his magic tricks. A wee bit o' daffery to mak folk laugh. Real warlocks are different."

"But can I go to see him, Mammie?" Betty still demanded.

"We'll see. Keep warm by the fire now and read yer school book – ye're comin on fine wi' the readin, the dominie tells me. I'll maybe let ye go to see the magician if yer coughin's stopped by Saturday night and if yer breathin's stronger."

While she was talking, Christina Sinclair was looking at Betty's reading book, turning each page slowly, gazing down at the mysterious lines of little black letters that made no sense to her at all. It seemed to her a miracle that Betty could actually read those words.

Although Henny was pleased that Betty was so much

better, she couldn't help feeling that something was still not quite right. Betty refused to let anyone question her about that terrible fall into the river. If Henny asked her why she'd gone so near the water or how she'd slipped on the bank, her face would go deathly white again. She would scream uncontrollably. Her hands would tremble.

"I canna remember a thing!" she would sob. "It's been all washed awa in the river."

"Henny, dinna pester the lass," begged her mother. "Just leave her in peace!"

By Saturday night Betty did seem well enough to go to see the famous conjurer who was coming from Glasgow. Henny wrapped her up well in two layers of warm clothes and tied a white scarf over her head. Then the family led her gently down the stairs and along to the Institute where the mill-hands were crowding into the Big Hall to see the magic tricks, willingly paying their penny each at the door. At one end of the hall, a high stage had been built from wooden boxes. The stage was bare except for one upright chair, one table hung with a black cloth that reached right to the floor, a long black box sitting on top of the table and an enormous glass jar on top of the box. The Sinclair family found seats in the fourth front row, right next to Rab. The hall buzzed with excitement. At last the conjurer himself stepped onto the stage and the mill-hands cheered. Henny had never seen a magician before. She gazed up at this odd-looking man. She felt unsure what kind of person he might be. He seemed kind enough, but perhaps he really was a terrible warlock after all.

The conjurer was tall and thin, dressed entirely in black, with a high top hat on his head. A long spangled cloak hung from his shoulders. Sparkling silver chains were draped around his neck. His drooping moustache, well oiled and curled up at the ends, made him seem utterly different from any man Henny had ever seen. His strangeness fascinated her. She stared and stared. He whipped off the hat with a flourish and bowed low to the audience, swirling his cloak around him. The people clapped and cheered. He bowed again. Then he led forward his assistant, a boy only about the same age as Rab but decked out in the most extraordinary suit of blue velvet with lace at the collar and wrists and pointed leather shoes on his feet. The boy began to play a merry tune on the tin whistle he held in his hand. Henny guessed at once what Rab would be thinking. He'd probably want to be a conjurer's boy himself and to go travelling all over Scotland in a fine horse-drawn carriage, moving on from town to town, playing his whistle at the start of each new act, holding his master's props for him and bowing to the crowd. But surely nothing in the world would ever persuade Rab to wear that ridiculous blue velvet suit! Henny wondered if the magician might take on a girl assistant. She wouldn't mind the blue velvet suit at all. In fact she thought she'd rather like it.

Then the magic tricks began. The audience sat breathless with amazement. Gold coins rose and fell in the glass jar, all of their own accord. The conjurer dropped an egg into a black bag, shook the bag upside down to show it was empty, and then suddenly produced the unbroken egg again from behind his assistant's ear. Tame white rabbits came and went with alarming speed in and out of the high top-hat. The conjurer could even read people's minds. He called this man or that woman up to the stage and told everyone the most amazing stories about their lives. How could he possibly know all those things? Were they true? The audience rolled about with laughter and the embarrassed man and woman went back to their seats with red faces.

Then the boy in the blue velvet suit took off his shoes and climbed bravely into the black box. To everyone's horror, the conjurer ruthlessly sawed his assistant in half, but then the boy stepped out of the box again without a mark on him. The people gasped in relief. They roared and clapped. Most astonishing of all, the magician waved his hands, murmured some magic words, and summoned up the shadowy shape of a small, white-faced child, hanging in the air above the table. Then with another wave of the magician's hands the child disappeared. The audience gasped. They roared and clapped again.

"It's all done wi' keekin-glasses!" Rab murmured to Henny with a knowing wink.

Henny shook her head. She had certainly seen that waif-like child hanging in the air.

"It was a ghost," she whispered to Rab. He laughed quietly to himself.

When the conjurer had finished and left the hall with his velvet-suited assistant and when his table and box and jar had been carried out to the waiting carriage, then the concert began. The village band played their instruments on the stage and the people lifted up their voices and sang lustily together. "Ye banks and braes" they sang and "The birks of Aberfeldy" and all the other old songs they loved. Then came the solos. One by one, a few brave souls climbed up on the stage to sing a Border Ballad or to recite a poem by Robert Burns. The audience joined in heartily with every chorus.

"Almost time to stop," shouted one of the overseers from the back row just before the mill-bell rang out its curfew. "Ye can have just one more song."

"One more song!" shouted the crowd.

To Henny's amazement, Betty was wriggling out of her seat and making her way to the stage. She was climbing the steps.

"Betty, come back!" hissed Henny.

"I'm goin to sing my song," Betty called back to her with a beaming smile.

When the crowd saw who it was that was standing on the platform, they cheered yet again. She must really be better, they thought to themselves, yon poor wee Sinclair lassie that fell into the river and was nearly drowned.

"This is my spinnin song," Betty announced and she launched straight into it, her voice ringing out clear and strong. The tune was one they all knew well, an old fishermen's tune from Caithness. But the words were new.

Spin, my spindles, spin,
Spin like the whirl o' the sea

Where the fisherman lies asleep
And never comes back to me.

Turn, my spindles, turn,
Turn like the swing o' the tide,
Where the herrin leap in the nets,
And boats to the harbour glide.

Fly, my spindles, fly,
Fly like the birds o' the wild,
Where the gannet dives to the wave,
And the kittiwake calls like a child.

Sing, my spindles, sing,
Sing like the birds o' the land
Where the women carry the peats,
And dream on the silvery sand.

Dance, my spindles, dance,
Dance in yer lang, white hair
Till winter comes to its end,
And geese climb high in the air.

There was a sudden hush in the hall when Betty had finished her song. Then tumultuous applause broke out. Men stamped their feet. Women wiped their eyes. Children shouted and called.

Henny and her mother looked at each other in silent amazement. Who had taught Betty that strange song? They had certainly never heard it before. And how could she be brave enough to stand up there and sing it in front of all those people? No-one else in the family could do such a thing. Betty was moving back to her place now, nodding and smiling at everyone who stretched out a hand to help her on her way. Christina Sinclair's face was a strange mixture of emotions, half proud and half embarrassed by her daughter's sudden fame.

"Who taught ye that song, Betty?" Henny demanded sharply as soon as her little sister had sat down beside her.

Betty seemed surprised.

"Naebody taught me the song, Henny," she said. "It just came into my head when I was sittin by our warm fire today. I was thinkin about all the spinnin machines in yon mill where our mammie works. I walked in there one day, ye ken, and I watched her spinnin till the overseer told me to get out. Maybe the spinnin machines gave me the words."

Henny laughed out loud. How could stupid machines tell Betty the words? The girl must be mad! Or had the magician cast a spell on her?

"Wheesht!" said Mother. "Come along hame, all o' ye. We'll get this poor child back to her bed. She's no quite her old self yet. We've maybe let her out too soon."

"It must have been the river that's changed her somehow," Henny murmured to Rab in a puzzled voice. "Or maybe it was the fairies that live in the river. She's forgotten everythin that happened to her on yon day she fell in the water but now she's suddenly found this song instead. Do ye think she made it up hersel?"

"Never!" said Rab. "She couldna! She's only a wee bairn."

· 157

"Then d'ye think she's fey, perhaps?" Henny asked him in horror. "Is she goin to dee?"

"Na, Henny!" Rab answered with a confident smile. "Betty's no goin to dee till she's an old, old woman! But ye could be right about the river-fairies. I think maybe they've touched her brain. She'll never be quite the same lassie she was before, will she?"

Henny shivered.

As the crowd moved out into the night and back to their houses again, everyone was singing Betty's song.

Spin, my spindles, spin,
Spin like the whirl o' the sea
Where the fisherman lies asleep
And never comes back to me.

CHAPTER 13

Nightfrost

New Lanark, November 1819

"Tonight's the night!" Rab whispered urgently as he caught up with Henny after work one icy-cold evening in November. He seemed to be strangely excited.

"What night?" asked Henny.

"The night for sclimmin over the wall!" Rab laughed. "The dark's come down already and the moon's big and bright. Look!"

"Rab, I'm never sclimmin round yon wall again," said Henny sternly. "After what happened to Betty, we canna risk yon mad swing over the water. We'd all be drouned like our faither."

"I've thought o' that," said Rab, grinning at her. "I kent you wouldna like to fly over the river so I've found a new way. I'll slip round the end o' the wall by mysel. Naebody ever gets drouned in my family! I'll take a lang rope wi' me and I'll gang further up the wall on tither side. I'll tie the rope to a big tree and I'll throw the end over the wall. Then ye can easy sclim up the rope and we'll baith be safe in the woods."

Henny was silent.

"But why tonight, Rab?" she said at last. "Any old night'll do for the woods. I'm stane-tired. I'm awa to my bed."

"Na, Henny. There's frost settlin on all the trees over there. And the moon's shinin down on the frost. I want ye to see it. The woods'll be lookin as if they're on fire. White, sparklin fire. Ye'll never forget it, as long as ye live."

Henny was tempted. She thought about the trees under frost.

"Aye," she said at last. "When?"

"After the curfew bell."

"Too late," she cried. "I'm no allowed."

"Yer mither willna ken, Henny! Wait till she's sleepin and all the wee bairns. Creep out, quiet as a mouse. I'll meet ye by the wall's end. The rope'll be ready." He ran off before Henny had time to protest.

A few hours later, when the village had fallen silent and her mother's breathing came and went gently, Henny pulled on her mill-clothes and a warm jacket. She crept out of the room.

Rab was waiting for her by the river. The moonlight lit

160

up his round smiling face and his spiky fair hair. His eyes seemed bluer than ever.

"This way!" he murmured and ran up the hill beside the wall to a point where his rope dangled down already from a tree on the far side.

"It's easy!" he said. He shinned up the rope, paused for an instant on the top of the wall and dropped out of sight. He threw the rope back again. Slowly Henny pulled herself upwards, her feet against the wall and the rope in her hands. This was far better, she thought to herself, than swinging out over the water. From a safe perch on the branch of the tree, she pulled the rope up towards her and let it hang down into the woods. She grabbed the rope and slithered to the ground.

"We'll run up to Corra Linn first," said Rab at once, running off under the trees. "The keeper's safe in his cottage tonight."

Henny sped after him, catching something of his strange excitement, but at the top of the next rise, she stopped abruptly, gasping in terror. Straight in front of her was a ghastly white thorn bush hung with dead moles and weasels, dead stoats and foxes, dead crows and badgers, each carcase touched with an uncanny silvery light.

"Rab! What is it?" cried Henny, clutching at his arm.

"The gibbet," said Rab grimly. "That's where yon keeper hangs up all the poor creatures he's shot or trapped. He thinks it'll be a terrible warnin to the ither wild beasts. He calls it his dool-tree."

Henny shivered. She certainly wouldn't like to be

caught by that keeper. She only hoped the man was safe by his fireside tonight and not roaming these woods with his dog. She turned her eyes away from the horrible sight. Her courage came flooding back again as she looked up at the tall bare trees, transformed by the sparkling frost, shining and glittering in the moonlight. Every black branch, every twig, was etched in silver.

"Come awa!" whispered Rab.

They ran swiftly through the woods and climbed the last slope to Corra Linn. Cold air rushed in and out of their lungs in icy gasps. On the high bank above the water they both stood still.

The waterfall was a tumbling white torrent. The mist was a silvery cloud in a starry sky. The river below them moved in a shining stream. The frozen trees held up their silent arms. This magic place, lovely as it had been in the green of summer, seemed to Henny even more astonishing now under the strange spell of frost and moonlight. She forgot the scary gibbet.

They darted up the steps to the hall of mirrors and sat there unconcerned for ten minutes or more as the dry white flood of reflected water seemed to pour down onto their heads. Henny laughed out loud as she sipped invisible silver tea from an invisible teacup. But Rab was eager to move on, locking the door behind them, taking a new track under the quiet trees as far as the badgers' sett. The minute they saw the black hole in the side of the sandy hill, they halted with a jerk of surprise. Three plump badgers were gambolling about in the moonlight, fossicking for worms in the undergrowth, snuffling at old yellow mushrooms and licking up red rowan berries that had fallen to the ground. The badgers came up close to Henny's feet, quite unaware of her presence, and then turned swiftly away again with a sudden flick of their necks.

"Look, Rab!" she breathed, pointing to the third badger. He was bigger than the other two, strong and powerful as he moved about on the hillside, but he limped awkwardly whenever one of his front paws touched the ground. He swayed and swaggered unevenly like an old sailor, home on land after many long months at sea.

"Our brock that was caught in the trap!" Rab whispered in delight.

In a mood of triumph they left the badgers to their play and made for the wall. Rab pulled himself up by the rope to the top and waited till Henny sat beside him. Before the moment came to skim down the rope, they peered through the bare, silvery trees and right down to the sleeping village of New Lanark. It lay so quiet, so still in the moonlight.

"Rab! What's that?" Henny asked him, startled.

"What's what?"

"There's a red light movin along the street by the mills. Look! Somebody's holdin a lantern. That's never allowed after curfew. He'll be in awful trouble."

"Likely it's just some overseer, makin sure everybody's in bed," said Rab with a laugh.

The distant red lantern seemed to tremble and shake as it moved. It passed by Number One Mill and then by

Number Two. Outside Mill Number Three it stood still. Then, as if a door had been opened and shut again, the light disappeared.

As they watched, the flickering light soon appeared again, a little higher up. It seemed to climb the stairs in Number Three Mill all of its own accord. Henny and Rab saw the faint red spot shimmering out from the windows of the first floor, then from the second and then from the third. Higher and higher it moved, until it shone from a window on the very top floor.

"Maybe he's searchin for somethin," suggested Henny. "Somethin up on my scutchin floor. Among yon bales o' cotton from far over the seas."

"He'll be comin down again soon, whoever he is," Rab said. But the little red light did not move down.

"Yon wee flame's gettin bigger," said Henny in surprise, a few minutes later. "Or maybe he's lightin up all the ither lanterns. But why would he do that in the middle o' the night?"

The light of the lantern did seem rather bigger. It glowed more fiercely. First one more window was red and then the next. Now all the windows on the top floor were glowing. Henny sniffed at the cold night air.

"Rab!" she cried in alarm. "Smoke! That's no lanterns we can see in the mill! That's fire!"

Quickly they slid down the rope, one behind the other, leaving it dangling behind them. They hurtled towards the village, fear catching at their throats, the stench of smoke stronger in their nostrils every minute. The houses lay asleep.

"Rab, ye must ring the mill-bell on Number One," Henny panted. "That way we'll wake the whole place up."

Rab rushed off. Henny stood alone at the foot of Number Three and gazed up at the fiery windows. At that very moment, with tremendous cracks like thunder, one pane after another on the top floor began to explode outwards into the night. Tongues of yellow flame licked out through the gaps and ran up the walls towards the roof. A hail of silver glass showered down to the ground, biting at Henny's face, scratching at her hands. She shrieked and scuttled away from the mill, her arms over her head, her eyes shut tight until she was well out of range. Black smoke was billowing from the shattered windows high above her. The fire was roaring up there like a maddened beast in a cage. Henny stared in horror.

"A face!" she cried, a new fear catching at her throat, but there was no-one near to hear her.

On the third floor of the mill, well below the raging fire, a terrified white face stared down at her.

"Who is it?" she gulped. "When will Rab ring that bell?"

As if in answer, the great bell clanged out its message at last, filling the whole valley with sound.

All along the rows of quiet houses, windows were flung open, questions were shouted. Then a terrified wild cry echoed around the village from every throat.

"Fire! Fire!"

The roof was burning now. Henny ran to the mill door. Someone must be trapped up there. The pale figure at the window was waving his hands in despair. He seemed to be shouting but Henny could hear no sound except the crackling of flames and the crash of the top floors collapsing. She pushed the door open a little but she did not dare to go in. The smoke caught at her throat.

"Rab! Rab!" she shouted out loud. "Stop yer ringin! I'm no sclimmin up these stairs all by my lane!"

The great bell stopped as if Rab had heard her. In a few seconds he stood on the step beside her.

"Na, Henny," he cried at once, pulling her violently backwards. "Ye canna gang in there!"

"We must, Rab!" she whispered. "Somebody's trapped! I saw his face at the window!"

Once in the dark interior, they were caught up in smoke. Acrid black smoke that filled their eyes, their noses, their mouths, their lungs.

"Pull off yer coat, Henny," Rab shouted to her, "and I'll pull off mine! We'll dip them in yon barrel o' water by the foot o' the stairs. Now, hang it all drippin, over yer head. That's the way! We'll crawl up the stairs on our hands and knees. Keep yer head verra low, Henny. Near to the steps. Smoke rises up high, ye ken, but there's aye a safe wee space close to the floor. My faither told me."

With wet coats over their heads, they crawled slowly up from step to step, their heads as low as they could manage. They were coughing badly but still breathing from the invisible trough of air. They passed the first floor, the second floor. They came to the third floor. The smoke was thicker here. From far below Henny could hear the shouts and cries of a growing crowd. She knew there was nothing those good folk could do with their pathetic buckets of water. There were no pumps at the mills, no hoses. The mill would be sure to burn to the ground even though a full and dancing river flowed past them all the while.

Rab pushed open the door of the long spinning room on the third floor. Cautiously, he and Henny lifted the wet clothes from their eyes and peered around them. A boy was lying on the floor, his body touched by moonlight. They almost lost sight of him as a new wave of smoke swirled in from the staircase. Then he swam into view again, lying completely still.

"Ye grab his feet!" Henny coughed out the words. "I'll tak his heid. We'll drag him feet-first down the stairs. Whatever's the matter wi' the poor lad? His eyes are starin in an awful strange way."

"Stop!" cried Rab. "We'll need mair help!" He ran to the window and broke the glass with one hand swathed in his wet coat. He bellowed down to the crowd below.

"Help! Help!"

He saw a group of astonished men rushing for the mill door.

"They're comin, Henny!" Rab called as he ran back to her. "Pull yer coat over yer head again and we'll start pullin this great lump of a boy, whoever he is!"

Henny grasped the boy's neck. Rab took his ankles. Blindly, with eyes and mouths shut tight, they edged their way to the door. Still trying to keep their heads low but choking on the smoke with every new breath, they pulled and bumped and dragged the heavy weight down the stairs from step to step. By the time they had reached the second floor they were exhausted. Their lungs were bursting. The smoke was overwhelming them. Henny fell heavily across the prostrate boy. Rab slumped on top of her. The men were pounding up the stairs.

In an instant, Henny was lifted into somebody's powerful arms. Rab was hoisted up to another strong man's shoulder. It took three more men to carry the unconscious boy, dragging him roughly between them. In a rush of terror, their mouths clamped shut as the smoke surged around them, the five men thundered down the last two flights of stairs and out into the open air where they could breathe again. The crowd surged forwards.

"Who is it?" hundreds of voices were crying. "What were they doin in the mill? Poor foolish bairns!"

"Stand clear!" bellowed one of the men. "Fetch the surgeon! Give them air!"

"The reek! The reek!" cried the crowd, tumbling backwards to get away from the smoke, staring in horror at the three lifeless bundles in the men's arms.

Christina Sinclair stood waiting in the crowd, cold with fear. Betty stood beside her. As soon as Christina saw Henny's familiar red hair, she knew exactly who it was. She rushed forward, screaming Henny's name out loud. The men had lowered all three bodies to the ground and were fanning them desperately with shirt or tunic, pressing down hard on their backs with spread hands, trying to pump fresh air into their lungs. Betty ran with her mother. She hardly paused to glance at Henny or Rab. She was gazing down in wonder at the third silent bundle. She was staring at a pair of pale eyes, half-open under heavy lids.

"Mammie!" she cried with a great smile of recognition on her face. "It's the big kind boy!"

CHAPTER 14

The Master Returns

New Lanark, November 1819

The stunned crowd stood and watched all night long as Mill Number Three burnt slowly to the ground. They stared up in horror as the fire devoured the roof timbers, red against a black sky. Then they saw the roof collapse onto the top floor with a great crash and a new explosion of sparks and flames. Now the fire roared in the wind. The top floor fell in its turn onto the one beneath, bales of raw cotton blazing, machines twisted by the heat and blackened by smoke, leather belts shrivelled and stinking. Hour by hour, fuelled by oil and cotton and wood, the fire in the mill spread slowly downwards as each burning floor dropped to the next, dragging everything with it.

It was the terrible sound of that fire that the mill-hands remembered for the rest of their lives. The flames howled in the night wind. The roar was deafening. Clouds of acrid black smoke filled the whole valley and crept up even as far as the Old Town where good folk rolled over in their beds and wondered what that strange smell could be. The intense heat of the fire was blown towards the silent crowd, singeing hair and beards, drying mouths, reddening the pale skin, making eyes run and sting, irritating the lungs to helpless coughing, forcing the people further back. But still no-one retreated to the houses. Frost melted to water on the nearest trees. A few damaged spinning mules were rescued at the very last minute from the ground floor. Nothing more could be saved.

By dawn, the mill was a blackened shell of stone with smoke still rising from the ruins. Even the rough outhouses near the river, where the master kept his new bales of cotton, had crumbled to ash.

As soon as he had eaten his breakfast, Donald Gillespie, the master's manager of the mills, climbed wearily to his counting house at the end of Caithness Row where the windows looked down onto the village square. He stood at his desk to write the terrible news to Mr Owen, far away in London. Once he had set down the bare facts of the fire, he went on:

We shall start immediately to work one of the other mills for twenty-four hours a day. I hope this plan will meet with your approval, sir. I suggest we let all the hands from the ruined Number Three Mill, men, women and children, take the night shifts in Number One. They can sleep by day. In that way they will lose no wages and we shall lose not even one day's production of yarn.

I very much hope, sir, that you will soon be back amongst us to claim insurance and to start on the plans for rebuilding. We have already begun to make enquiries about how the fire could have started up on the top floor of Number Three and what those three children were doing in the mill at midnight. One of them, the girl, is from that troublesome Sinclair family that came south from Caithness in July. I suggest we send the whole family back to Wick. Another is the son of John Cunningham, the clockmaker. An excellent workman, as you often say, sir, but a man of strange and dangerous ideas. In my humble opinion he is a Luddite, a Radical and a revolutionary and I strongly suspect that young Robert Cunningham has been infected by his father's wild talk. The boy may well have lit the fire as a deliberate attack on your splendid mills and machines. He is certainly the most likely suspect. The other boy is Dan Drysdale, your housekeeper's nephew, who worked in your own garden until you moved him to the mills. He is quite seriously injured by smoke and cannot yet answer any of our questions but the surgeon says that all three children are likely to recover well after some weeks of rest. I shall, of course, leave all decisions about their future to you, sir.

Everyone in New Lanark is deeply shocked by this tragedy. May I respectfully suggest, sir, that things would be much better for us here if you could return to New Lanark as soon as possible. The poor hands are always much easier to manage when they know you are at the mills. They rightly put great trust in your fatherly presence.

I remain, sir,
Your respectful servant,
Donald Gillespie, Manager.

When Mr Owen arrived back from London, he immediately set about probing into the cause of the fire. He couldn't help being impressed by Rab Cunningham's full and honest account of why he and the Sinclair girl had been in the mill at all, though he was astonished to discover that the two of them had dared to go trespassing in the Bonnington woods in the middle of the night, and not for the first time apparently. He hardly thought it possible, but both of them told the same extraordinary story with so many details about the waterfall, the hall of mirrors, the keeper's gruesome gibbet and some poor wounded badger. They couldn't have invented it. They finally convinced the master that their first glimpse of the fire had been from the top of a wall they should never have climbed.

"I will give you just one more chance at New Lanark,

Rab Cunningham, and you too, Henny Sinclair," he had said to them at last after a painful interview. "If there is even one more breach of my rules, both of you will leave the mills at once and your families will go with you. You are never to go over that wall again! Do you understand?"

Rab and Henny had nodded. Rab knew he would have to find some new paths and new woods where he and Henny and Jockie could wander on Sunday afternoons, somewhere that was not forbidden by the master's rules or the law of the land. It wouldn't be easy to find such places. But perhaps the old Roman Road might be a good start or the old fort at Castledykes or the little Mouse Water. Perhaps he'd even lead them to the secret Tree of Liberty one day, hidden away in its woods. Henny sighed. For her, no other place could ever be quite as good as the world over the wall.

Mr Owen had rather more difficulty in getting Dan Drysdale to talk. Dan's lungs were badly damaged by smoke, though no skin or hair was burnt. It was sheer terror and terrible choking breath that had kept him penned in that spinning room on the third floor for so long while black smoke poured down the stair-well from above. The boy had been paralysed by fear. His aunt was the only one who could get much sense from him now. Bit by bit, over the next few days, she pieced together his miserable tale and passed it on to the master. Dan had been angry and bitter, she explained, because he hadn't been given the work he'd expected in the Braxfield household. That was the kernel of the whole thing. When

Jockie had been appointed to the place Dan regarded as his own by right, the older boy had first tried to get rid of his rival by attacking him in the coal-house, but Jockie had bounced back from that blow on the head and poor Dan had been banished to stair-sweeping. Next he'd hoped to drive the whole family home to Caithness by pitching the younger girl into the river. They'd never stay in New Lanark, he thought, if the silly child was drowned. But the girl had somehow survived her fall into the water and the family had not left. In final desperation, he'd decided to threaten the master himself. That, at least, would be a kind of revenge. He'd never meant, or so he said, to burn down the whole mill. It was entirely an accident. He'd only wanted to start a small fire on the top floor, opening up his oil lamp and holding the yellow flame to one of the bales of cotton. He just wanted to give everyone a fright. Above all else, he'd hoped to be the one to ring the bell, to give the alarm, to be thanked by a grateful master. But the fire had leapt out of control. It was as simple as that.

When Mr Robert Owen had heard the whole story from Miss Drysdale, he sat by himself at Braxfield House with his head in his hands. Dan Drysdale really had gone too far this time. It was not the boy's own fault, of course. The poor lad had learnt those violent emotions and that wild destructive behaviour from his ignorant parents. Always the same old story. Only if he could manage to mould the characters of children from the very day of their birth would he be able to change human nature! It was clearly far too late to change Dan now. The master knew he couldn't possibly risk keeping him on at the mills. The hands wouldn't put up with it, for one thing. Dan Drysdale would have to be brought to justice or there might be another fire, a worse fire, a fire with loss of life. The master knew that there was no course open to him but to take the boy before the Sheriff as soon as he was well enough to walk. Dan would be sure to be convicted of arson and sent to prison or even transported to the colonies. Transportation might be better, the master thought to himself. A grim, harsh life, of course, but one with the chance of a new beginning when the boy had served his time. Dan Drysdale might come to some good yet.

When Henny had fully recovered from the fire and started back at her work in the mills, she spoke quite suddenly to Rab one Sunday afternoon as the two of them set off together to explore the old Roman Road.

"Rab, I'm only waitin till I'm sixteen or seventeen, ye ken. Then I'll be leavin these mills. I'll be gangin back hame to Wick."

Rab was completely silent.

"Jockie likes it here, I ken that," she burbled on. "He likes the steady work and plenty to eat. A warm house and a good maister. And maybe he'll be a fine butler one day. He's aye askin me what mair I could want."

"What mair is it that ye're wantin then, Henny?" Rab asked her with his old smile.

Henny was not sure what she was wanting but she knew there was something. Perhaps she longed simply for the sea itself, the mysterious sea that was always pulling at her heart. Or perhaps she needed the old familiar place where her father might seem closer. Or perhaps she was drawn by the work she would do there, a fresh herring in one hand and a knife in the other. But one thing was certain. She wanted to go home. And surely Betty would want to leave the mills and go with her. Betty's song had shown everyone that her heart was still in the far north.

Henny glanced suddenly at Rab as a new thought darted into her mind. Perhaps one day Rab himself might travel north to that little blue harbour at Wick. He might even get to like the place. Who could tell?

As for Jockie, on a cold Sunday afternoon in December he brought a new treasure down to the village for his mother to see.

"Just look at this, Mammie!" he cried excitedly, waving a story-book close to her face. "One of the maister's bairns gave it to me! He says he disna need it any mair. He's got a bigger one with mair pictures. But he says this is good enough to start with. Listen to me readin, Mammie!"

Jockie stood on a chair and opened the book.

"I was born in the year 1632," he read slowly in a loud and solemn voice, all on one note, "in the city of York, of a good family, though not of that country, my father being a foreigner of Bremen, who settled first at Hull."

"What is it, Jockie?" shrieked Betty, jumping up and down and trying to see the words on the cover.

"*Robinson Crusoe*!" cried Jockie in triumph, leaping

from his chair. "And I'm goin to keep this book for ever and ever! Our maister says it's the best book in all the world. Much better than the Bible, he told me this mornin!"

"Goodness gracious! What a shockin idea!" cried Christina Sinclair with a gasp. "What would yer dear faither say if he could hear ye now, Jockie? But Mr Owen's a kind maister so perhaps ye should listen to him. Ye'll maybe need to read both the good books, my Jockie. The Holy Bible and this Robinson person, whatever its tale might be. What ye canna find in one story, ye'll maybe find in tither."

She took the book from him. She opened it up and gazed in wonder at the black-and-white picture on the very first page. She saw an odd-looking man, dressed in the skins of wild animals. His hair was long and his beard unkempt. He seemed to be standing by a lonely seashore, his eyes fixed in amazement on a footprint in the sand.

Then she turned to the lines of type. Those small black marks on the page that Jockie could read so easily were still a mystery to her. Suddenly, Christina Sinclair had a powerful longing to read this strange little book for herself.

"In the New Year, Jockie," she said, smiling down at him, " I'm comin with ye to the night-school!"

Glossary

Scots words and technical words connected to the cotton trade

ain	own
anither	another
awa (rhymes with caw)	away
ay/aye	yes
aye/ay	always, continually
babby	baby
bairn	child
baith	both
bane	bone
beck	bow, curtsey
birk	birch tree
bittie	a bit, a small piece
blae	blue
blaeberries	bilberries
blether	talk foolishly, gossip
blethers!	nonsense!, rubbish!
bobbin	a wooden or metal cylinder with a hole at each end so it can fit onto a spindle and spin. Cotton thread is wound onto a bobbin in the spinning process.
bonny	beautiful, pretty, handsome

brae	hillside, steep path
braw	brave, fine, splendid, excellent
breeks	trousers
brither	brother
brock	badger
byre	cowshed
canna	cannot
card	an English word – to comb cotton by machine to prepare it for spinning
chantie	chamber-pot
clarty	dirty, muddy
coo	cow
cop	an English word – a conical ball of thread, wound on a spindle in a spinning machine
couldna	couldn't
crack	a good talk or a friendly gossip with someone
creepy	a low stool
daffery	fun, foolish behaviour
daft	foolish, crazy
day-daw	daybreak, dawn
dee	die
deid	dead
din	a loud noise
ding	knock or strike with heavy blows
dinna, disna	didn't, don't, doesn't
dis	does
dominie	schoolteacher
douce	sweet, pleasant, lovable, respectable
doun	down
drap	drop
drouned	drowned

easy	easily
faither	father
fash	trouble, bother
feardie	coward
feart	afraid
fecht	fight
fey	fated to die, as shown by strange behaviour; other-worldly
flue	wisps of cotton fluff in the air
fossicking	searching, hunting about for something
gab	talk idly, volubly
Gaelic	Celtic language spoken in Scottish Highlands
gang	go
gie	give
gin	trap, especially to catch wild animals
glen	steep-sided valley
Glesca	Glasgow
gloamin	dusk, evening twilight
goller	shout, roar, yell
grandchilder	grandchildren
greet	weep or cry
gruesome	horrible
guid	good
haar	cold sea-fog
hailsome	healthy
hairmless	harmless
hame	home
heid	head
hissel, hersel	himself, herself
hurlie-bed	bed on wheels

injine	engine, machine, *see also* 'Jeanie'
isna	is not
ither	other
itsel	itself

Jeanie, Jenny	an affectionate name for the spinning machine; probably does not come from the name of the inventor's wife, as was once thought, but from a shortened form of ingine or engine. Engine became Ginny which in turn became Jeanie or Jenny.

keekin-glass	mirror
ken	to know
kent; weel-kent	knew, known; well-known
kilt	skirt, part of male Highland dress
kin	kinsman, relation, related to
kirk	church
kist	chest or large box

lad, laddie	boy
lade	*see* mill-lade
lane, on yer lane	lone, alone, by yourself
lanely	lonely
lang	long

Lanimers, Lanimer Day

the day of holiday and celebration in the town of Lanark, still kept every year on a Thursday between the 6th and 12th June. It celebrates the annual 'Riding of the Marches' when the whole population of Lanark rides or walks in procession to make sure that every boundary stone (or landmark

182

	– Lanimer) of the town is safely in position. Many other towns in Scotland and England have a similar annual ceremony, but only in Lanark is the day called 'Lanimers'.
lap	an English word – a flat sheet or layer of cotton fibres, ready to be fed into the carding machine
lassie	girl
linn	waterfall
lowp	leap, jump
mair	more
maister	master; owner, boss; the term often used for Mr Robert Owen, master of the New Lanark Mills
maistly	mostly
mak	make
Mammie	mother (child's word)
midden	pile of rubbish
mill-lade	a fast-flowing channel of river-water directed under a spinning mill in order to turn the water-wheel and so operate the machinery; below the mill, the lade flows back into the river
minnie	mother (child's word)
mirk	dark, darkness
mischancie	risky
mither	mother
the morn	tomorrow
mule	a kind of spinning Jenny, invented by Samuel Crompton in 1797
murtherer	murderer
mysel	myself

na/nae	no
naebody	nobody
naethin	nothing
the necessary	outside toilet
no	not
och aye	yes
ony	any
oorie	gloomy, dismal, uncanny
peerie	a child's spinning top
peevers	flat stones used in hopscotch; the game of hopscotch
perfit	perfect, perfectly
pick	in weaving, to throw shuttle across the loom
piecer	an English word – in spinning, one who mends or joins broken threads
pirn	a bobbin, a spool on which yarn is held after spinning, ready for weaving; also, the yarn itself, wound onto a spool by the spinning machine
portion	a passage chosen from the Bible for reading aloud at family worship
privy	outside toilet
puddock-stool	toadstool, mushroom
redd up	cleaned up, tidied up
reek	smoke
riggin	arrangement of masts and sails on a ship
rovin	a loose rope of raw cotton (a sliver), drawn out and slightly twisted, ready for spinning
rubbage	rubbish

sair	sore, hard to bear, distressed
sapsie	soft, lacking courage
sark	shirt
scavengers	those who clean up rubbish
sclim	to climb
Scots	the language of Lowland Scotland
scutchin	cleaning raw cotton before spinning
shinty	a game rather like hockey
sic	such, so
skelp	to strike, hit
sky-settin	nightfall, sunset
slivers	an English word from the spinning industry. It means a continuous band of loose, untwisted fibres of cotton, ready for drawing and roving. It can be pronounced to rhyme with either 'shivers' or 'divers'.
smitch	a small speck
sodger	soldier
souter	shoemaker, cobbler
spindle	a revolving rod which twists cotton fibres into thread
stane	stone
stane-tired	very tired
stang	throb with pain, to ache
swander	become giddy or faint, to stagger
swee	a movable iron bar over a fire, on which kettles, pots etc. can be hung
swirl	a whirling movement of water, a whirlpool
tak	take
tak tent	take notice of someone or something
theirsels	themselves
thrum	beat or strike

tingle	ring or chime
tither	the other
toun	town
troon the school	play truant from school
trow	believe
ugsome	disgusting, horrible
verra	very
warlock	a wizard, magician, a man who is thought to bewitch people
warp	in weaving, the strong threads stretched lengthways in a loom
wat	know
water-frame	a spinning machine operated by water-power
wasna	was not
wean	a young child
wee	small, tiny
weel; weel-kent	well; well-known
weft	in weaving, the threads that cross from side to side, weaving in and out of the threads of the warp
wheesht!	hush!
wi, wi'	with
wifie	wife
willna	won't, will not
wouldna	would not, wouldn't
yella	yellow
ye	you (singular and plural)
yer	your, you're
yersel	yourself
yon	that one or those over there